目 录
CONTENTS

中国新疆名胜古迹 PLACES OF HISTORIC INTEREST AND SCENIC BEAUTY IN XINJIANG, CHINA

高昌故城

ANCIENT TOWN OF GAOCHANG

坐落在火焰山下的高昌故城
The ancient town of Gaochang at the foot of Flaming Mountain

高昌故城鸟瞰
A bird´s eye view of the ancient town of Gaochang

高昌故城一隅
A corner at the ancient town of Gaochang

高昌故城位于新疆吐鲁番市东45公里、吐鲁番县东南40公里处火焰山南麓的木头沟河三角洲，是古代高昌回鹘王国的都城遗址。全盛时期的高昌城地理位置十分重要，是闻名遐迩的古丝绸之路的必经之地和重要门户，在中西交往史上产生过广泛而深远的影响。虽然经过2000多年的风吹日晒，沧桑巨变，历史上的繁华都市已不可重见，但故城轮廓犹存，城墙气势雄伟，巍然屹立于火焰山下。1961年，高昌故城被国务院列为全国重点文物保护单位。

The ancient town of Gaochang was once the capital city of the Gaochang (Kocho, Kharakhoja or "King City") Uigur Kingdom. Lying at the Mutougou River Delta at the foot of Flaming Mountain, 40 km southeast of Turpan County, or 45 km east of Turpan City of the Xinjiang Uygur Autonomous Region, Gaochang served as an important commercial and cultural center on the ancient Silk Road and played an important role in the history of communication between ancient China and the West. The once thriving capital city basically returned to the surrounding desert as more than 2,000 years passed, but the outline of the ancient town is still visible and the city wall still stands below the Flaming Mountain. The ancient town of Gaochang was listed as a key cultural relics unit under the state protection in 1961.

高昌故城残存的高大城垣
Ruins of the high city walls of the ancient town of Gaochang

高昌城历史悠久，始建于公元前1世纪，是西汉王朝在车师前国境内的屯田部队所建，因其“地势高敞，人广昌盛”（《北史·西域传》）而命名“高昌”，中国汉、魏、晋历代均派有戊己校尉驻此城，管理屯田，故又被称为“戊己校尉城”。高昌城地区历史上战乱频仍，其管辖权曾在几个不同的少数民族之间数度易手。公元327年，前凉张骏在此置高昌郡，继之又先后为前秦、后凉、西凉、北凉所控制。442年，北凉沮渠无讳在此建立了政权。450年，沮渠安周攻破交河城，灭车师前国。公元460年车师国亡，柔然立阚氏伯周为王，称其国为高昌国，掀开了高昌王国的序幕。

Gaochang was initially constructed during the first century BC, by the troops of the Western Han Dynasty (206 BC-25 AD) which garrisoned the Anterior State of Cheshi (an ancient state in Central Asia) for the purpose of exploiting the wasteland and growing food grain. According to historical records, the city was situated on a high and vast piece of land and had a large population, hence the name Gaochang (a high and prosperous city). From the Han to the Jin Dynasty (206 BC – 420 AD), troops were sent by the ancient Central Governments to garrison the city and manage the farmland, so it was also called the Garrison City.
Gaochang suffered form conflicts and chaos and was ruled by several ethnic minorities during its history. In 327, Zhangjun, king of the Former Liang State established Gaochang County here. The city was subsequently controlled by rulers of the Former Qin, Later Liang, Western Liang and Northern Liang states (376 - 403). In 442, Juqu Wuhui of the Northern Liang established his state in Gaochang. In 450, Juqu Auzhou broke through and occupied Jiaohe City, the capital of the Anterior State of Cheshi. In 460, Avar helped Kan Bozhou become the king after completely conquering the Cheshi State and the newly-born kingdom was named Gaochang.

火焰山下的高昌故城
The ancient town of Gaochang at the foot of Flaming Mountain

故城上的晾房（左）
Air-curing barns in the ancient town of Gaochang（Left）

吐鲁番民居（右）
Residence in Turpan（Right）

故城内烽火台
The beacon tower in the ancient town

佛塔
Pagoda

拱门
Archway

佛寺僧房
Monk´s dwelling houses

建筑结构
Building structure

楦构造的土坯墙
Adobe walls with shoe last structure

吐鲁番高昌故城遗址

Ruins of the ancient town of Gaochang in Turpan

吐鲁番高昌故城

The ancient town of Gaochang in Turpan

高昌故城一角

A corner of the ancient town of Gaochang

此后高昌城区发生了无数次征战，13世纪中叶以后，天山以北广大地区的蒙古游牧贵族以海都、都哇为首发动叛乱，多次侵犯回鹘高昌国，高昌城在战争中遭受严重破坏，满目疮痍，面目全非。公元1275年，蒙古军士12万人围攻高昌，战争持续达40年之久，高昌终于在战乱中被毁，自此便逐渐被废弃，一座历史悠久的古城彻底退出了历史舞台。

Hereafter Gaochang was successively attacked by other ethnic groups. During the mid-13 century, the nomadic Mongolian aristocrats, lead by Haido and Dowa, started rebellions and trespassed on the Gaochang Uigur Kingdom time after time, as a result Gaochang city was damaged severely and lost its former prosperity. In 1275, a Mongolian troop of 120,000 soldiers besieged the city and the warfare lasted 40 years. Thus, the once thriving capital city of an important kingdom was destroyed eventually and vanished into history.

高昌故城城墙

The city walls of the aancient town of Gaochang

高昌故城远眺

Looking at the ancient town of Gaochang from afar

高昌故城鸟瞰
A bird's eye view of the ancient town of Gaochang

汉唐以来，高昌是连接中原、中亚、欧洲的枢纽。经贸活动十分活跃，世界各地的宗教先后经由高昌传入内地，毫不夸张地说，它是世界古代宗教最活跃最发达的地方之一，也是世界宗教文化荟萃的宝地之一。鼎鼎大名的唐代佛教高僧玄奘西游时就曾经经由高昌，在此诵经讲佛，传法布道，并与高昌王结拜为兄弟，留下了一段千古佳话。

Gaochang long served as an economic and trade hub connecting the Central Plain, Central Asia and Europe since the time of the Han and Tang Dynasties (206 BC - 907 AD). Religions from all over the world were introduced into the Central Plain through Gaochang by merchants from home and abroad. Honestly speaking, Gaochang was one of the most important religious centers in the world at that time. It boasted various religious cultures. It is said that Xuanzang, the renowned Buddhist monk-traveler of the Tang Dynasty (618 - 907) gave lectures in Gaochang on his pilgrimage to India in search of Buddhist sutras. He established a strong friendship with the king of the Gaochang Kingdom.

高昌故城房屋遗址鳞次栉比，可以想见当年的繁华
The ruins of the ancient town of Gaochang show that on either side of the roads were row upon row of houses, which remind people of the magnificence of the city in the past

高昌故城　The ancient town of Gaochang

现存的故城遗址，是高昌回鹘时期在唐代高昌城的基础上建设而成的，全城呈不规则正方形，总面积约220万平方米，城市布局大致与唐长安城相仿，在历经多年建设后形成这样的规模，它主要有三部分组成：

外城：外城城墙轮廓基本完整，部分地段保存极好，周长约5.4公里，城墙基厚12米，高达11.5米。每面有2－3座城门，其中西面靠北的城门保存最为完好，有曲折的瓮城和大量的马面，均为夯土筑成，夯层厚8到12厘米，间杂少量的土坯，有极清晰的夹棍眼，外城的东南和西南部分，还可以看出有寺院的遗址。故城外城是搊氏高昌时期所建。出土文书中有“论块中城”、“东南坊”、“西南访”等记载，说明当时此城已有外、中之分，东、南、西、北之别，并有各城门的名称，如：青阳门、会德门等，同时在唐代西州时期还有子城。

The ancient town site we see today was constructed during the period of the reign of the Uigurs in Gaochang on the bases of the old Gaochang city left behind from the Tang Dynasty. The new city, an irregular square in shape, covered an area of 2.20 million square meters. The general pattern of the city was similar to that of the then Chang'an City of the Tang Dynasty. After successive construction for many years, the complete scale which can still be somewhat seen came into being, which was comprised of three parts: the outer city, the inner city and the palace city.

The wall of the outer city is fairly well preserved, with some sections being remarkably so. The city wall had a perimeter of 5 kilometers and was 12 meters thick and 11.5 meters high. Two or three gates were built in each side of the wall, of which the northern gate in the west side is best preserved. The wall was made of rammed earth, which was 8-12 centimeters thick and occasionally reinforced with adobes. In the southeastern and southwestern parts of the city are some relics of temples. The outer city was built during the period of the reign of the Qu in Gaochang. According to historical documents, Gaochang City, at that time, was divided into outer and inner cities, each with four sides. The gates in all four directions each had a name, including Qingyang Gate, Huide Gate. A satellite town was constructed when it was under the jurisdiction of the West Prefecture of the Tang Dynasty.

高昌故城城墙
The city walls of the ancient town of Gaochang

外城城墙　The city walls of the outer city

内城佛塔

Pagoda at the inner city

内城：内城居外城正中，即外城的中间，宫城的南面。城墙全为夯土筑成。西、南两面的城垣大部分还保存下来，间有破坏的地方，东面只能看到东北角的高地与东南角的一个土台基，北面正中和西北角还有一部分残垣基地，至于城门的遗址从地面上一点痕迹也找不到了。据测算，内城周长约3600米，和《隋书》中的记录基本一致。其建筑年代较外城早，平面呈南北长方形，内城主要是宫城和寺院建筑等。

内城城墙
The city walls of the inner city

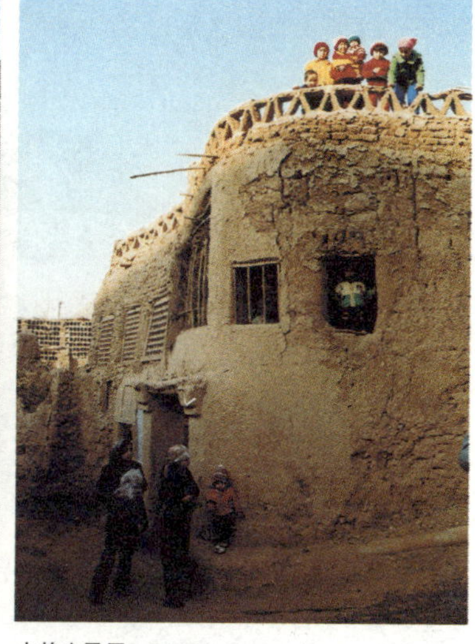

火焰山民居
Residence in the Flaming Mountain

The inner city sat in the middle of the outer city, south of the palace city. Its walls were made of rammed earth. Most sections of the south and west sides are well preserved. On the east side only a raised area at the northeastern corner and an earth platform at the southeast corner are left. Some of the base of the collapsed wall in the middle and at the northwestern corner can be seen. The sites of the gates in these two directions cannot be found any more. It is estimated the perimeter of the inner city is approximate 3,600 meters, which basically accords with the one recorded in the *History of the Sui Dynasty*. The inner city was built earlier than the outer city. It is rectangular in shape with the distance between south and north being longer than that of east to west. The inner city held mainly the palace city and temple complex.

内城凹入地下的双层建筑

Two story building with semi-underground first floor

内城民居

Residence in the inner city

内城

The inner city

内城作坊

Workshops in the inner city

东面内城墙体

The city wall to the east side of the city

内城城墙

The city walls of the inner city

内城墙

The city walls of the inner city

佛塔基座

The foundation of the pagoda

瓮城内城墙上有残留壁画的洞穴

A cave with remained frescoes at the city walls of the jar city

禅舍

Buddhist abode

宫城遗址 Ruins of the royal palace

城中之宫城 The royal palace in the city

故城墙体
The city walls of the ancient town

宫城居全城最北部，外城的北墙是宫城的北墙，内城的北墙是宫城的南墙。整个宫城平面呈长方形，周长约700米，西墙还有几处残基，连接起来，可以看出遗迹。东墙完全被破坏，什么也看不到了。宫城内留存下的许多高大的殿基，一般高3.5米至4米左右，夯层厚度约35–48厘米，可以看出是一座高达四层的宫殿建筑遗址。早期的宫城在今“可汗堡”内。麴氏高昌时期随着外城的修建，宫城迁迁至北部，南面而王，与隋、唐时长安城的布局相似，回鹘高昌时期宫城曾大动土木。

The palace city was situated in the northernmost part Gaochang city. Its north wall was part of the outer city wall and the south wall was part of the inner city wall. The city shaped like a rectangle and had a perimeter of some 700 meters. The site can be vaguely identified according to the remnant base of the west wall, while the east wall has vanished completely. There are many rammed earth bases of a ruined palace which was as high as four stories. The bases are 3.5-4 meters high and 35-48 centimeters thick. The palace city was initially located inside the Khan’s Castle. It was moved north during the construction of the outer city during the period of the reign of the Qu in Gaochang. The layout of the city was similar to that of the then Chang’an city of the Tang Dynasty. The palace city experienced large-scale construction during the period of the reign of the Uigurs in Gaochang.

墓道 Tomb passage

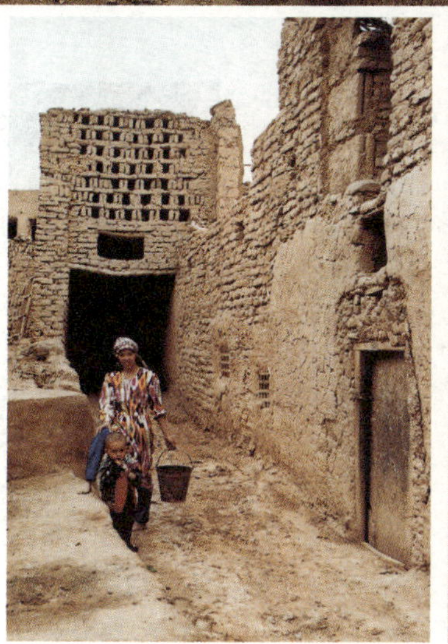

吐鲁番民居建筑阁楼
The attic in the residence of Turpan

遗落在内城池中的陶牛
The clay cattles found in the inner city

王室寺院，传说唐朝著名高僧玄奘西天取经途中曾在此讲经说法
The royal temple, where it´s said that the eminent Buddhist monk, XuanZang, in Tang Dynasty ever gave lectures on his way to India

讲经堂的大门
The main entrance to preaching hall

高昌故城现存多种名胜古迹，是为其一千多年沧桑历史的见证，比较著名的有以下几处：

一 相传为唐僧讲经处的佛寺 位于外城西南角，是全城最大的佛寺遗址。佛寺的佛龛内还有菩萨像和壁画。据考证，这里就是当年唐僧讲经之处。讲经台旁还残存着一座高15米的佛塔，正面的一座佛像现在只留有两只脚。侧面有许多佛龛，称“万佛塔”，原来应该是有许多小佛像雕塑。

The ancient town of Gaochang is richly endowed with places of historical interest and scenic spots, which witnessed its rises and falls during its history. The most famous places include: the Buddhist temple, Khan's Castle and tomb complex.

The Buddhist temple, lying at the southwest corner of the outer city, was the largest Buddhist temple in the city. The niches in the temple house sculptures of Bodhisattva and some are decorated by murals. Evidence suggests that the famous Xuanzang once taught here on his way to India. Beside the platform where Xuanzang gave lectures, there stands a 15-meter high pagoda. One of the sculptures of Bodhisattva on the front side of the pagoda only has the two feet remaining. There are many niches on the sides of the pagoda for small sculptures, hence the name of Ten Thousand Pagoda.

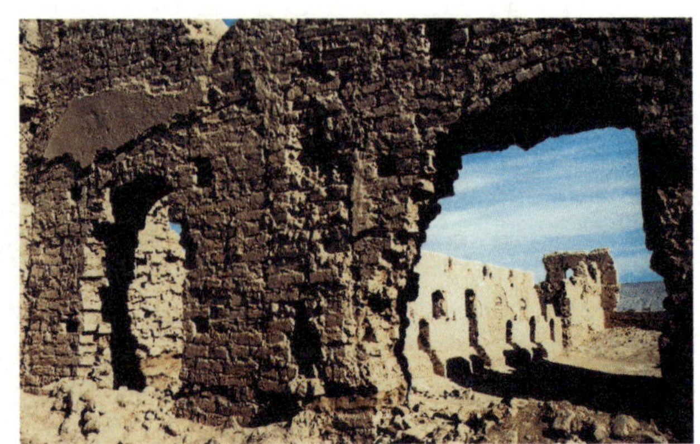

佛寺外围附属建筑
The peripheral buildings of the temple

墓道

Tomb passage

加固的支体

Counterfort walls

故城北路

The north road of the ancient town

讲经堂内景

The interior of the preaching hall

故城西南方的佛寺讲经堂（下左）

The preaching hall in a temple located in the southwest of the ancient town. (lower left)

高昌故城是全国重点文物保护单位（下右）

The ancient town of Gaochang is under special protection of the national government. (lower right)

二 可汗堡 是一处疑似唐朝宫殿的遗址，位于内城北部正中，当地人称之为“可汗堡”。堡内北面的高台上有一高约15米的塔状建筑物；西边还有一座建筑物，分为地上地下两层，现仅存地下部分，南、西、北三面有阶梯式门道供出入，其与交河故城现存的唐代官署衙门建筑形式相同，可能是一宫殿遗址。

The Khan's Castle is guessed to have been a site similar to the palaces of the Tang Dynasty (618-907). The palace is situated in the middle of the northern part of the inner city, which was called Khan's Castle by the local residents. On the high terrace in the northern part of the castle stands a tower-shaped building 15 meters high. Somewhat to its west, a half-underground, two-storey building is supposed to be the palace ruins. On its south, west and north sides are ladder-style gateways. The construction pattern of the building is similar to the yamun (government offices in ancient China) left behind from the Tang Dynasty (618-907) in the Ancient town of Chohe.

高昌背靠的火焰山
Gaochang with the Flaming Mountain at the back

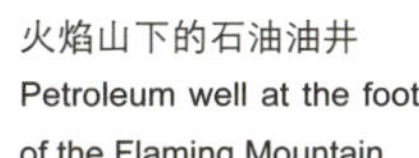

火焰山下的石油油井
Petroleum well at the foot of the Flaming Mountain

营房遗址

Ruins of barracks

火焰山下的村庄
Village at the foot of the Flaming Mountain

吐鲁番村庄里的清真寺
The mosque in Turpan village

三 城北墓葬群 是高昌故城居民们的墓地，位于高昌城北的一片戈壁，城内居民死后大都葬在这里。整个墓群占地10平方公里左右。这里曾出土文书、织物、墓志、钱币、泥塑木雕俑、陶木器皿、绘画、农作物、瓜果食品等各种历史文物。

总之，高昌故城自公元前1世纪（西汉）建"高昌壁"到13世纪末（元初）废弃，使用了1300多年。它不仅战略地位重要，为历代兵家必争之地，而且也曾是古代西域重要的政治、经济、文化中心之一。高昌为连接中原、中亚、欧洲的枢纽，经贸往来活跃，同时，各种宗教先后经由高昌传人内地，是世界宗教文化荟萃地之一。这里出土的多种文字的古代文物，是研究西域历史和文化的重要史料。

城墙上的防御设施

Defenses on the city walls

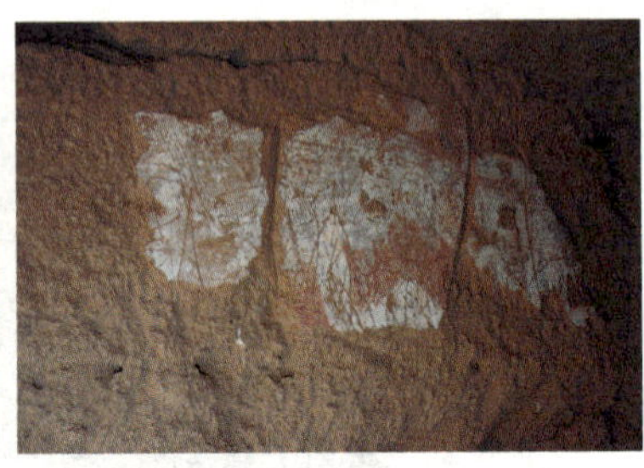

佛龛内残留的壁画

Remained frescoes in a niche

The tomb complex is located north of Gaochang City on the Gobi desert. It was the public cemetery of the ancient Gaochang residents. The tomb complex covers an area of 10 square km. Among the cultural relics excavated there are books, textiles, epitaphs, ancient coins, clay figurines and wood sculptures, pottery and wood wares and paintings.

Generally, the ancient town of Gaochang, from the original construction of Gaochangbi (Gaochang Wall) in the first century BC (in the Western Han Dynasty from 206 BC-25 AD) to its desolation at the end of 13 century (at the beginning of the Yuan Dynasty (1206-1368)), had experienced a history of more than 1300 years. Gaochang was a place of strategetic importance, as well one of the political, economic and cultural centers in the ancient Western Region. Gaochang served as a transport hub connecting the Central Plain, Central Asia and Europe. Religions worldwide were introduced into the Central Plain through Gaochang by the merchants from home and abroad. Gaochang was one of the most important religious centers in the world. The multi-language cultural relics excavated are important materials for studying the history and culture of the ancient Western Region.

从瓮城可看到烽火台

The beacon tower is visible from the top of the jar city

带有夹棍眼的商铺

Shops with distinctive stick holes at the walls as a result of earth ramming

北庭都护府

PROTECTORATE BEITING

北庭都护府故城遗址是新疆维吾尔自治区重点文物保护单位

Ruins of the Protectorate Beiting is now put under the special protection of the Xinjiang Uygur Autonomous Region

外城北门　North gate to the outer city

北庭都护府是唐朝时期（618—907）设立于西域的特别行政机构。其遗址位于新疆吉木萨尔县城以北10多公里的北庭乡境内，又称“破城子”，是全国重点文物保护单位。

The Protectorate Beiting, the special administrative organ in the Western Region, was established in the Tang Dynasty (618-907). The relic site is situated in Beiting Township more than ten km north of Jimsar County, Xinjiang Autonomous Region. Also called “Pochengzi (the Broken City)”, it is one of the Cultural Relics of National Importance under the Protection of the State.

北庭历史上曾是“挟千里以超里海，筑伟业而壮三军”的西域重镇。2000多年的历史长河中，北庭先后为塞人、车师、粟特、柔然、突厥、回纥、蒙古等多个民族所居住，从公元前59年由西汉中央政府建制的车师后国，到公元703年唐朝设置的西域最高行政管理机关和军事指挥机关北庭都护府，位于吉木萨尔县中部平原地区的这座故城，历经宋（960—1279）、元（1271—1368）的繁荣，是当时新疆的政治经济中心、丝绸之路新北道的重要枢纽。

Beiting is a historically famous town in terms of strategic significance. Over the past 2,000 years, Beiting had been inhabited by many ethnic groups such as Saka, Cheshi, Scythae, Avars, Turk, Uighur and Mongolian. In 59 BC, the central government of the Western Han (206 BC-8 AD) established the Posterior state of Cheshi in Beiting. In 703, the central government of the Tang Dynasty (618-907) established the Protectorate Beiting there, as the highest administrative and military organ. It was located in the central plain of Jimsar county. As the political and economic centre of Xinjiang at that time, as well as a major transport hub of the new north route of the Silk Road, Protectorate Beiting prospered during the Song （960-1279）and Yuan（1271-1368）Dynasties.

北庭故城护城壕
Entrenchments of the ancient city of Beiting

北庭都护府故城城墙现已有了保护措施
Measures have been taken to preserve the city walls of the Protectorate Beiting

故城西门
West gate to the ancient city

敌台　Battlements

西域重镇北庭

北庭的历史可以追溯到春秋战国时期（前770—前221）。据记载，由塞人组成的天山六国当时就已定居在这里。西汉（前206—公元25）初期，北庭成为车师后国的王庭，故称后庭。汉宣帝神爵二年（前60年），西汉政府设立西域都护府后，于此设金满城。

Famous Town in the Western Region

As early as the Spring and Autumn Warring Period (770 BC-221 BC), the six kingdoms of Tianshan Mountain comprised of Saka had settled in Beiting. In the early period of the Western Han Dynasty (206 BC-25 AD), Beiting served as the state capital of Posterior state of Cheshi, also called Houting. In the second year of the Han Emperor Xuanwu named Shenjue (60 BC), the central government of the Western Han Dynasty built Jinman City here after the establishment of the Western Region Protectorate.

北庭古城最早出现于南北朝（420—589）的西突厥时期。中亚历史上著名的商业民族——粟特族用骆驼横跨了中原、新疆和印欧地区，并在这里建立了自己的商品集散中心。突厥人将其命名为“可汗浮图城”，即北庭古城的雏形。

The Beiting Ancient city emerged in the Western Turks Period of the Northern and Southern Dynasty (420-589). The Scythae Ethnic Group, historically famous businessmen in central Asia, set up their own trade center, using camels for transport, to connect the central plain, Xinjiang and Asia and Europe. The Turks named it “Khan Buddha Town”, which is the original city of Beiting.

北庭故城内城　The inner city of ancient Beiting

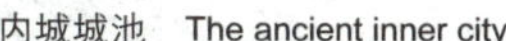

内城城池　The ancient inner city

北庭故城残存的高大城垣　Ruins of the high city walls of Beiting

北庭都护故城城墙
The city walls of Protectorate Beiting

In the 12th year of the Emperor Zhenguan of the Tang Dynasty (638), the Western Turks was divided into two Khanates. Yipiduolu Khan established his capital here and it became "Beiting", and Yipishapoluo Khan set his capital in the south in "Nanting". In the fourteenth year of the Emperor Zhenguan of the Tang Dynasty (618-907), the central government of the Tang established Tingzhou prefecture, which exercised jurisdiction over three counties including Jinman, Pulei and Luntai. Later, Jinman County was renamed Houting County.

唐贞观十二年（638年），西突厥分裂为两个汗国，乙毗咄陆可汗的牙帐在北，乙毗沙钵罗可汗的牙帐在南，号称“北庭”、“南庭”，北庭之名由此而来。贞观十四年（640年）唐王朝置庭州，辖金满、蒲类、轮台三县，后金满县改称后庭县。

城内到处都是破碎的花砖瓦当，显示古老的历史
Broken bricks and tiles found everywhere in the ancient city tell the long history of Beiting

702年，武则天为了加强对西域的管理，在北庭设立北庭都护府（后升为大都护府），置瀚海军，管辖包括天山以北和巴尔喀什湖的广大地区，最远的管辖范围达里海东部。当时的北庭古城人口稠密，经济繁荣，是“丝绸之路”上重要的交通枢纽和军事要冲。北庭都护府的地位也相当于现在的乌鲁木齐，首任大都护杨何的品级也达到了从二品，相当于现在的副总理一级，这是北庭最为辉煌的时期。自此之后北庭城垣修葺扩建，规模宏大，历代享有盛名。

In 702, the Tang Empress Wuzetian established the Protectorate Beiting (upgraded to the Grand Protectorate later) here to strengthen its administration over the Western Region. The Protectorate Beiting had a vast area under its jurisdiction including the northern area of Tianshan Mountain, the Balkhash Lake area, as far as the eastern area of the Caspian Sea with the Hanhai Army stationed there. At that time Beiting had a dense population and enjoyed economic prosperity, as a major transport hub in the Silk Road and a military strategic area. The status of Beiting at that time equaled present day Urumqi. The first official of Protectorate Beiting, Yanghe, appointed by the central government, was granted Second Official Rank, which is equal to the vice premier. This was Beiting's most splendid period. Afterwards, the walls of Beiting were repaired and enlarged. Beiting was well known over ages.

高大的城垣依稀可见当年北庭都护府的雄姿

The high city walls remind people of the magnificence of the ancient Protectorate Beiting

外城　Outer city

城池 Inner city

北庭城池 Fortress of ancient Beiting

北庭故城南北长1500米，东西宽约1000米，周长4590米，分内外三重。第二重南北长600米，东西宽400米。第三重边长各200米。外城城墙宽7—10米，版筑土夯成。内城墙厚3—5米不等，高约7米。内外城分设南、北、西三门，相互贯通，北门为正门。内城设都护府衙署，第二重为市街，外城驻瀚海军及部分居民。城东西两侧各有天然河道，宽200米，至北门西侧合二为一，形成月牙状一湾湖水，可荡舟泛棹。湖边烟柳花色，奇丽多姿。

The ancient city of Beiting was 1,500 meters form south to north, and about 1,000 meters from east to west, its perimeter totaling 4,590 meters. The city was divided into three sections by walls, outer, middle and inner. The second wall is 600 meters long form south to north, and 400 meters wide from east to west. The outer wall has the same side length being 200 meters.The outside wall is seven to ten meters thick, built with rammed earth. The inner wall varies in width from three meters to five meters, and is about seven meters in height. All inner and outside walls had south, north and west gates. The north gate served as the main gate. The office of the magistrate was in the inner city, and the second section was the street and the market, and the outer city was the Hanhai Army garrison and a residential area. There were rivers to the east and the west of the city, each about 200 meters wide. The two rivers met at the west side of the north gate, forming a crescent shaped lake with beautiful willows and flowers on the banks.

北庭城内多楼台花木，庙宇恢弘，人民善于冶金雕玉，百业兴旺。畜牧业尤其发达，多名马，以毛色分群放牧。人民富裕安宁，贫苦者也以肉为主食。在北庭的北山（今卡拉麦里山）中出硇砂，白天烟气如云雾，夜间火光照见禽兽，大地呈赤彩色，极为壮观。

北庭植物园
The Botanical Garden of Beiting

北庭商贸城正门　Front gate to the Beiting Business Town

The inner city of Beiting abounded with buildings with balconies, flowers and trees, as well as a large temple. People were skilled at metallurgy and jade sculpture. All industries were booming. Animal husbandry was well developed and produced many famous horses. The horses were divided into different herds by their hair color for breeding purposes. The people enjoyed a rich and peaceful life; even the poor had meat as their staple food. Salmiac was in the mountain (the present Karamori Mountain) north of Beiting. The smoke of the salmiac looked like clouds or fog in the day time, while at night it was so bright that people could see the wild animals in the distance. It dyed the ground red, very spectacular.

北庭文化广场上介绍北庭史的石碑
Stone tablet recording the history of Beiting at the Beiting Cultural Plaza

文化广场的雕塑——北庭园
Beiting Garden, a sculpture at the Cultural Plaza

北庭作为大唐帝国天山北麓的军事、政治中心，与天山南麓的安西大都护府南北辉映，光照史册。唐代著名诗人岑参曾生活于北庭，留下了许多传唱千古的名篇，为北庭这座历史名城留下了珍贵的影照。

As the military and political center in the north of Tianshan Mountain during the Tang Dynasty, Beiting earned its place in history. So did the Anxi Grand Protectorate in the south of Tianshan Mountain. The famous Tang poet Censhen lived in Beiting and wrote many masterpieces. His poems are a treasure of Beiting.

故城外围的红花
Safflowers（Carthamus tinctorius L.）outside the ancient city

Beiting was called Bechbaliq during the Yuan Dynasty, which followed the name of that the Posterior State of Cheshi had five cities in Han Dynasty. Genghis Khan sent a Darughachi (an official title in Mongolian) to govern Beiting and stationed a large military force there, taking it as the secondary capital. In the first year of the Emperor Xianzong of the Yuan Dynasty (1251), a Minister of the Province (the highest official of the Province was entitled the Minister rank) was set as the highest administrative organ in Bechbaliq, as well as the 11 provinces in the central plain. In the 23rd year (1286) Yuan Dynasty, a Marshal Office was set in Beiting.

元朝称北庭为别失八里，也是沿袭汉代车师后王庭有五城之地的俗称。成吉思汗在这里设达鲁花赤（意为监临官、总辖官）进行管理，并驻扎重兵，又把它作为陪都。元宪宗元年（1251），设别失八里行尚书省，与中原11行省同时设立，为地方最高行政机构。至元二十三年（1286），别失八里设都元帅府。

北庭街心花园
Street garden in Beiting

明永乐十年（1412），北庭古城毁于战火。永乐十六年（1418），明政府遂将政治中心迁往亦力把力（故址在今伊犁），北庭自此衰落，并最终在中国历史上销声匿迹。

In 10th year (1412) of Emperor Yongle of the Ming Dynasty, Beiting was destroyed in a war. In the 16th year (1418), the central government of the Ming Dynasty (1368-1644) moved the political center to Yili bal (the present Ili). Beiting declined, and finally it disappeared.

北庭西大寺外景

The exterior of the Beiting West Temple

城外的护城壕沟
Entrenchments outside the city

正在进行维修保护的北庭西大寺
The Beiting West Temple is under renovation

北庭故城遗址

1771年，清朝大学士纪晓岚在吉木萨尔的城郊意外地发现了一座已经废弃的古城，当地人称之为“护堡子破城子”。查遍史料及在古城中发现的遗迹，纪晓岚认为，这座古城就是史料记载中早已湮没的北庭都护府所在地。他还细心测量了城墙砖的大小，留下了“厚一尺，阔一尺五六寸，长二尺七八寸”（1尺=10寸≈0.33米）的原始记录。这是北庭古城于明代废弃后首次见于文字的记载。

The Ruins Site of Beiting

In 1771, Ji Xiaolan, the Great Scholar of the Qing Dynasty, discovered a deserted city in the urban area of Jimsar County, which was called “Hupuzi Pochengzi” (broken city) by the locals. Upon searching historical records and studying the relics discovered in the city, Ji Xiaolan thought that the ruin was the location of Protectorate Beiting which had been long since passed into oblivion. He also measured the wall brick, and wrote down the original record of “about 0.33 meters thick, 0.5 meters wide, and 0.9 meters long”. That was the first written records about Beiting after it was abandoned during Ming Dynasty.

北庭故城文化新城广场

Xincheng Cultural Plaza of Beiting

北庭故城遗址至今轮廓清晰，内外三重城墙尚可辨识。残垣断壁断断续续，最长处不足百米。北城墙厚约7米，最厚处可达10米。城垛高台和角楼遗痕20余处，最高的达12米。城内洞屋相连，大者深5米，宽约3米，高3米；小的深3—4米，宽约2米，高2.5米。洞房均为拱顶，长方形。个别洞屋有套间，呈连环状。其中三座大洞屋内正墙中各有佛龛。故城第二重东城墙城垛内也有一个5米多深的洞室，与北城墙洞室相同。一般认为这些洞室为当年瀚海军住所。城内坑穴遍布，地表浮土约10厘米，盐碱很浓，生长有爬地蔷薇、骆驼刺、芨芨草、蓬蒿及地衣等植物。故城中当年遗留下来的街市塔庙、衙署、外城角楼、敌台等遗迹，有的轮廓仍依稀可辨。随处可见破碎的瓦砾、陶片。

北庭故城中出土了很多有价值的文物，主要有唐代石狮、铜镜、莲花纹方砖、瓦当、开元通宝等。

The site of Beiting city has a clear outline now, with the three identifiable walls. Crumbling walls and dilapidated houses can be founded here and there. The longest crumbling wall is less than 100 meters. The north wall is about seven meters thick, and the widest wall is10 meters in thickness. There are more than 20 battlements and turrets, among which, the highest is about 12 meters. The houses and caves in the city were connected to each other. The larger ones were five meters deep, and about three meters in width and height. The smaller ones were about three or four meters deep, about two meters wide and two and half meters high. The cave and the house are shaped in rectangle with an arched roof. Some caves and houses had interlinked rooms. On the north wall there are three large caves each of which contains a Buddhist niche. There is a cave room which is more than five meters deep in the eastern wall of the second wall. It was said that these cave houses were the dwellings of the Hanhai Army. Pits and tunnels can be found everywhere with the ten cm of loose earth, which contain a high salt content. There are roses, alhagi sparsifolia, achnatherum splendens, celery wormwoods and lichen. Within the city are the ruins of the street, market, towers, temples, offices, the turret of the outside city, battlements, parts of them have recognizable traces. Broken bricks and pottery pieces are all over the city.

Many valuable cultural relics have been excavated in Beiting, such as the stone lions of the Tang Dynasty, copper mirror, and square bricks with lotus patterns, eave tiles and Tang Dynasty coins.

生长在护城河边的植物——苦豆子

Sophora alopecuraides by the city moat

北庭千佛洞正门

Front entrance to the Thousand Buddha Grottoes

北庭千佛洞北门

The north gate to the Thousand Buddha Grottoes

北庭西大寺和千佛洞

在距离北庭都护府仅数百米的地方，有一座被农田所包围的古寺，因其与北庭都护府的附属关系，被称之为“北庭西大寺”。随着北庭古城的消失，它的生命似也走到了尽头，直到20世纪80年代才再次被发现。

Beiting West Temple and Thousand-Buddha Grottoes

Only several hundred meters from the Protectorate Beiting, an ancient temple was surrounded by fields. It was called “Beiting West Temple” because of its association with Protectorate Beiting. With the disappearance of Beiting City, the temple also came to an end. It was not discovered again until 1980’s.

北庭西大寺是高昌回鹘王室寺院遗址。回纥（回鹘）人迁到北庭城后，受唐风的影响、逐渐将原本信奉的摩尼教改为佛教。而且，高昌回鹘王国在信奉佛教的初期，主要利用旧唐寺和摩尼教寺院作为宗教场所。遗址中残存的壁画、佛像以及所表述的宗教故事，都生动反映了民族宗教的演变过程，是极为少见的存在于西域地区的宗教艺术景观。

北庭千佛寺大门
The front gate to the Beiting Thousand Buddha Temple

北庭千佛寺侧殿
The side hall of the Beiting Thousand Buddha Temple

Beiting West Temple was the site of the royal temple of the Gaochang Uighur. The Uighur believed in Manichean originally. Under the influence of the Tang Dynasty, the Uighur converted to Buddhism. In the early times, the Uighurused the old Temple of the Tang Dynasty (618-907) and the Manichean Temple to hold religious activities. Both the fresco and figures of Buddha remaining in the ruins and the religious stories reflect the conversion process. These are rare religious art masterpieces of the Western Region.

千佛洞内的观音菩萨像
The statue of the Goddess of Mercy at the Thousand Buddha Grottoes

北庭千佛洞卧佛
The reclining Buddha at the Beiting Thousand Buddha Grottoes

据史料记载，北宋（960—1127）时期，中原与当时的高昌回鹘关系密切，宋太宗派供奉官王延德等为首的100余人出使高昌国。高昌国狮子王当时正在北庭避暑，得知这一消息后在北庭隆重迎接了王延德。其间，他还陪同王延德参观了北庭西大寺。

北庭西大寺共三层，有正殿、配殿等，正殿部分已经坍塌。主殿部分的镶金佛像壁画的绘画技巧明显具有唐代风格。

According to historical documents, the Northern Song Dynasty (960-1127) saw a close relationship between the central plain and the Gaochang Uighur. The Emperor Taizong sent a diplomatic mission comprised of more than 100 people headed by the sacrificial offering official Wang Yande to Gaochang. The Lion King of Gaochang was in Beiting, the summer resort. Hearing the news, he met Wang Yande ceremoniously in Beiting. During Wang's stay in Beiting, the Lion King accompanied him to visit Beiting West Temple.

The Beiting West Temple has three floors, the main hall and wing hall. Most parts of the main hall had collapsed. The painting skills, used in the fresco of the golden figure of Buddha of the main hall, obviously are in the style of the Tang Dynasty.

吉木萨尔县千佛洞，位于吉木萨尔县城西南5公里处的天山山脉北麓的千佛山上。清乾隆三十五年（1770年），有民人避雨洞内而被发现。佛洞门为半月形，内有赤脚大卧佛一尊，身长5米有余。还有众多铜佛像，大小不等。有研究者认为应是宋使王延德自高昌至北庭途中休憩的高台寺。目前千佛古洞仅存卧佛，洞中发现的九尊铜佛现珍藏于北京故宫博物院。

The Thousand Buddha Grottoes in Jimsar is situated in the south-western area of Thousand Buddha Mountain about five km from Jimsar County north of Tianshan Mountain. In the 35th year (1770) of the reign of Emperor Qianlong of the Qing Dynasty, a farmer happened to discover it when he went in the cave to escape the rain. The Buddha Grottoes has a lune gate. It boasts a five meters high lying Buddha with bare feet and other copper figures of Buddha in different sizes. Some researchers think that was the Gaotai Temple where Wang Yande, the emissary of the Song Dynasty, rested on the way from Gaochang to Beiting. Currently, there is only the lying Buddha in the Thousand Buddha Grottoes. The nine copper figures of Buddha discovered there are in the Palace Museum in Beijing.

千佛洞内景
The interior of the Thousand Buddha Grottoes

北庭千佛洞壁画
Frescoes at the Thousand Buddha Grottoes in Beiting

北庭故城文化新城广场上晨练的人们

Morning exercises at the Beiting Xincheng Cultural Plaza

北庭商贸城街景

Street at the Beiting Business Town

中国新疆名胜古迹 PLACES OF HISTORIC INTEREST AND SCENIC BEAUTY IN XINJIANG, CHINA

哈密回王墓

THE MAUSOLEUMS OF THE UYGUR ROYAL FAMILY IN HAMI

哈密回王墓位于新疆哈密市回城乡，是清代哈密回王及其王室成员的墓葬建筑群。当地维吾尔族人称“阿勒同勒克”，意即“黄金之地”。

The Mausoleums of the Uygur Royal Family, located in the Huicheng Township, Hami City, Xinjiang Autonomous Region, are the tomb complex of Uygur kings and royal family members. The place of the mausoleums is called “Alatonlak” in the Uygur language, which means the place of gold.

哈密回王墓外景

The exterior of the Mausoleum of the Uygur Royal Family in Hami

独特的汉、蒙、满、维建筑风格

Unique combination of Han, Mongolian and Manchu architecture

哈密回王墓坐落在哈密市南郊回城乡的阿勒屯村

The Mausoleum of the Uygur Royal Family is located at the Aletum Village, Huicheng Township in the south suburb of Hami City

哈密回王墓棺椁
The inner and outer coffins of the Mausoleum

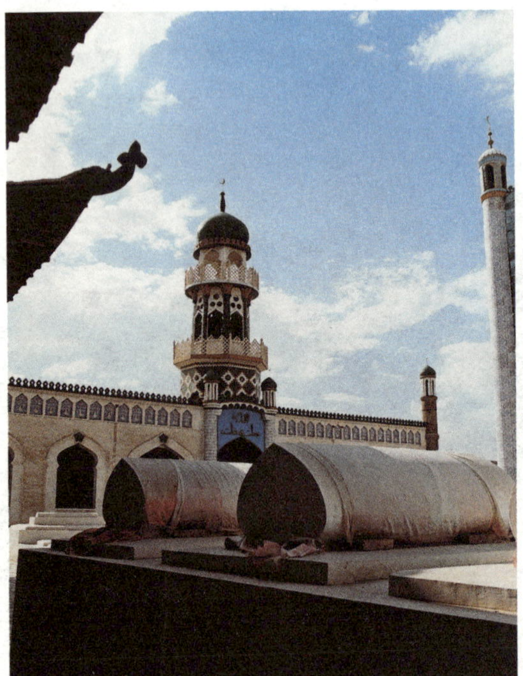

暮色中的回王墓
The Mausoleum of the Uygur Royal Family in the twilight

哈密回王是清政府对哈密地方封建领主赐予的封号。1697年哈密地方维吾尔首领额贝都拉因助清廷平定葛尔丹叛乱有功，被康熙帝册封为“一等札萨克达尔罕”，其部被编为镶红回旗，爵位世袭，由王公、贝子、贝勒一直晋封至亲王。其中第四世玉素甫被封为郡王，第七世伯锡尔死后被谥封为和硕亲王。又因清代伊斯兰教被称为回教，新疆建省前被称作回疆，信仰伊斯兰教的民众被称为“回部”，所以维吾尔藩王被称为“哈密回王”，回王府管辖区域为巴里坤以外的哈密地区全境和鄯善。

The Uygur King, also called the Hui King, is the title of the feudal lord of Hami, granted by the government of the Qing Dynasty (1644-1911). In 1697, by dispatching troops to help the Qing government to quell the Geerdan rebellion, Erbeidula, the local Uygur leader of Hami, received the honored title of “Top Jasagh Darhan” from Qing Emperor Kangxi. The forces under Erbeidula were organized under the bordered red banner of the Uygur with the hereditary titles from Wanggong, Beizi, and Beile to Prince. Yusupu, the fourth Uygur King, was granted as Junwang and Bosir, the seventh Uygur King, was granted as Prince Heshuo after his death. Islam was called “Huijiao” (the religion of the Hui ethic group), Xinjiang before establishment was called “Huijiang” (the frontier inhabited by the Hui ethic group) and the local people believing in Islam were referred to as the tribe of the Hui ethic group in the Qing Dynasty, so the Uygur Fanwang (a vassal king) was also called the Hui King in Hami. The Hui King exercises his jurisdiction over Shanshan and Hami except Barkol.

王爷府全景图
The panoramic view of the king's palace

一世回王额贝都拉像（1697-1709）
The portrait of the 1st Uygur king, Erbeidula (1697-1709)

哈密回王墓局部　One area in the Mausoleum

哈密回王墓建筑局部　One area in the Mausoleum

哈密回王墓墓室外景　The exterior of the coffin chamber

哈密回王一世额贝都拉，受封于清康熙三十六年（1697年），当时并不是王，而是一等达尔罕。直到1813年第七世伯锡尔承袭爵位时，才晋升为“亲王”。1930年传至第九世沙木胡索特时，因沙木胡索特的去世而爵位终止。从额贝都拉至末代沙木胡索特历传9代，共233年。

Granted in 1697, the 36th year of the Qing Emperor Kangxi, the first Uygur King Erbeidula was then not a king but a Top Darhan. He was not promoted to Prince until 1813 when the seventh King Bosir succeeded to the hereditary title. The hereditary title was ended in 1930 because of the death of the ninth King Samohosot. The title of the Uygur King descended through nine generations from Erbeidula to Samohosot with a history of 233 years.

三世回王额敏（1711-1740）
The 3rd Uygur king, Ermin (1711-1740)

七世回王伯锡尔（1813-1867）
The 7th Uygur king, Bohier King (1813-1867)

米克里·巴努- 8 世回王的母亲"亲王福晋"是实际的主政者（8 世回王是瘫王）
Minuli·Banu, the mother of the 8th Uygur king. This Qin Wang Fu Jin (Wife of Prince) was the actual ruler as the 8th Uygur king was paralyzed

9世回王沙木胡索特盛世(1881-1930)图景

A painting depicting the heyday (1881-1930) in the reign of the 9th Uygur king, Shamuhusuote

哈密回王为何能受朝廷倚重，从仅为平民之上的札萨克一等达尔罕晋升为“王”呢？哈密回王又为什么能得到当地维、汉等民族人民的尊敬，他们的故事又为什么在民间广为流传呢？这是因为历世哈密回王为维护祖国统一、民族团结、制止分裂和内乱立下了汗马功劳，所以历来受到清朝中央政府的信任和各族人民的爱戴。

Why were the Uygur Kings relied on by the Qing government? Why were the Uygur Kings promoted to King from Darhan which ranked only above civilians? Why were the Uygur Kings respected by the local Uygur and Han ethic groups? And why were their stories widely spread among people? All is due to their great contributions in supporting the Qing government by safeguarding the national unity and preventing divisiveness and internal strife. That is why they were always believed by the Qing government and held in great esteem by the people of all ethic groups.

从哈密回王一世额贝都拉起，哈密回王家族世代支持清政府屯垦戍边，参与剿灭准噶尔叛乱，平息大小和卓之乱，击退浩罕人侵，收复疆土，立下战功无数。《清史稿》记载：“哈密论战守功晋秩亲王。比于诸蕃有大勋于国”。

现存的墓室只有7至9世的尚存，其他墓均在露天

The extant coffin chambers are for 7th to 9th Uygur kings. The other tombs are in the open air

Starting with the first Uygur King Erbeidula, the Uygur kings of all generations supported the Qing government's practice of stationing troops to cultivate and guard frontier areas. They rendered outstanding service to the country by suppressing the Junggar rebellion and the rebellion of the Horji brothers who declared to be offspring of Muhammud, repelling the Khanate of Kokand aggression and reoccupying the border areas. Praise bestowed on the Uygur Kings' great feats was recorded in *The Draft of Qing History*.

台吉墓（首相）顶很像清廷的宫帽

The top part of the Taiji (prime minister) tomb resembles an official cap in Qing dynasty

7世、8世回王墓室门楼

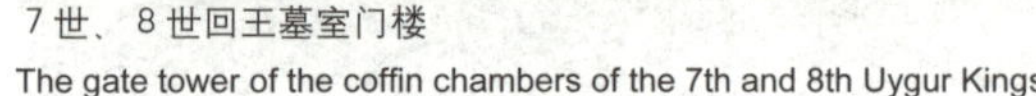

The gate tower of the coffin chambers of the 7th and 8th Uygur Kings

回王墓大门局部

The main entrance to the Mausoleum of the Uygur Royal Family

哈密回王墓，实际上是从1813－1930年间9世回王中最后三位名副其实的“哈密王”的陵寝，也就是额贝都拉家族第七至九世成员的墓葬地。

In fact, only three Kings among the nine generations of the Uygur Kings from 1813 to 1930 were buried in the Mausoleums of the Uygur Royal Family. Specifically, it is the burial ground of the seventh to ninth generations of Erbeidula's family.

台吉墓内景（上）
The interior of the Taiji tomb (up)

台吉墓天花板图样（下）
The ceiling decorations in the Taiji tomb (down)

回王墓占地1.3公顷，可分三部分。第一部分就是七世回王伯锡尔的大拱拜，埋葬着七世回王伯锡尔和八世回王默哈莫德王族40多人。

The Mausoleums of the Uygur Royal Family occupy an area of 1.3 hectares with three sectors. The first sector is a big tomb for the burial of the seventh Uygur King Bosir and the eighth Uygur King Muhammad and 40 royal family members.

2007年重修的哈密王府外景
The exterior of the Palace of the Uygur Kings, which was rebuilt in 2007

王府坐落在"回王墓"西侧
The Palace is located to the west side of the Mausoleum

第二部分，即伯锡尔拱拜南边的亭式木结构的小拱拜。据说原有小拱拜5座，现仅存2座，一座是末世回王沙木胡索特生前给自己修建的坟墓，一座是台吉墓。末世回王墓下部分为四方形，外部为用亭柱支撑的中原式亭榭结构八角攒尖顶，墓室笼罩其中。亭上飞檐起脊，状如华盖。内部是土坯垒砌的伊斯兰式的穹窿顶墓室，壁刷白粉，印蓝色祥云团花。此墓中葬有沙木胡索特，及其王室成员、王族等13人。

台吉墓下部是土坯砌墓室，上有亭柱支撑一木制构的充檐盔顶。墓中埋葬王室重臣台吉等，共12人。这两座墓以伊斯兰之穹窿顶为基础，吸收了中原汉族八角楼攒尖顶和蒙古式盔顶风格，是当地多民族文化交流的产物，在伊斯兰陵墓建筑中别具一格。

The second sector, located to the south of Bosir's tomb, is a small wooden tomb with a pavilion-type structure. It is said that there were five small tombs in the past, but only two of them are well preserved. One is the tomb of the last Uygur King Samohosot, built for himself during his lifetime. The other one was built on a pedestal. Looking from outside, Samohosot's tomb was built on a square base. On the top is a pavilion roof with octagonal upturned eaves, featuring the pavilion style of the Central Plains. With upturned eaves and ridge roll, the pavilion roof, supported by pillars, envelops the tomb like a baldachin. Entering the tomb, an Islamic style appears with a domed top built of adobes and the white walls painted with floral patterns of blue auspicious clouds. Samohosot and 13 royal family members are buried in this tomb.

The other tomb was built on an adobe pedestal. Supported by some pillars, a helmet-type wooden roof with double eaves envelops the tomb. Some 12 royal important officials were buried here. On the basis of an Islamic vault, the two tombs blend the Central Plains style of the pavilion roof with the octagonal upturned eaves and the Mongolia style of the helmet-type roof. The two tombs are the result of multi-national cultural exchange and have a unique style among the architectures of Islamic mausoleums.

回王清真大寺
The Id Kah Mosque

清真寺的内景，据说是新疆室内容量最大的清真寺
The interior of the Mosque, which is said to accommodate the most people indoor in all the mosques in Xinjiang

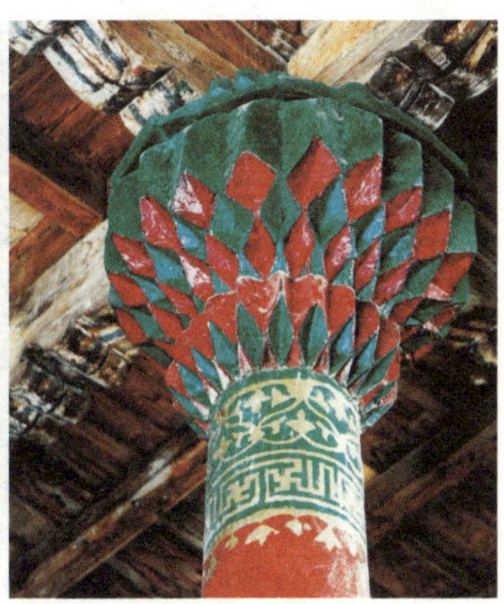

清真寺内的雕花木柱共108根
The 108 sculptured wooden pillars in the Id Kah Mosque

第三部分是艾提卡大清真寺。一进入寺内，就看到104根大红柱，像森林一样支撑着巨大的平面寺顶。木柱顶部刻有菱形和万字图案，寺顶彩绘藻井图案，墙壁粉白，书写有古兰经文，井间有花草衬托。寺顶开有天窗。寺顶外部设有唤礼楼。整个建筑紧凑严密，庄严肃穆，加之是平顶，确为独特的伊斯兰清真寺。

艾提卡清真寺可容纳5000人，每年肉孜节和古尔邦节，城乡穆斯林云集于此，诵经礼拜，虔诚之至。

The third sector is the Id Kah Mosque. Upon entering the mosque, a forest of 104 red pillars supports the huge flat roof. With pillars carved with diamond-type patterns and the pattern of a swastika on the top, the colorful ceiling with caisson pattern, the white walls with the Koran, the flowers and grasses in the patio, the windows in the ceiling, as well as the Huanlilou building on the outside, the mosque was designed with compact arrangement and solemn atmosphere. Especially with the flat top, it is indeed a distinctive mosque in design.

The Id Kah Mosque has a capacity of 5,000 persons. During the Id al-Fitr Festival and Id al-Kurban Festival each year, Muslim practitioners coming from cities and towns gather here, reciting scriptures and praying with great piety.

王府角楼上看“王爷清真寺”

Looking at the mosque from the turret of the palace

清真寺是典型的汉式建筑

The mosque is a typical Han architecture.

节日的回王大清真寺

The Id Kah Mosque in the festival time

清真寺内壁上的阿拉伯文经文
The scripture in Arabic language on the wall of the Mosque

宣礼塔内景
The interior of the minaret

大清真寺门前的宣礼塔外景
The exterior of the minaret in front of the Mosque

7世、8世回王墓室是典型的伊斯兰风格
The typical Islamic style coffin chambers of the 7th and 8th Uygur Kings

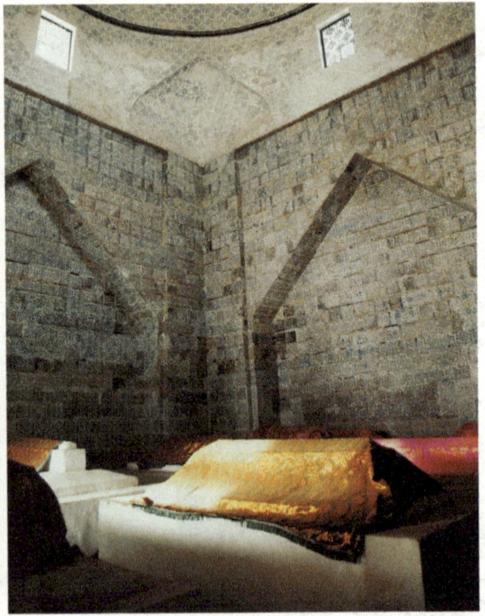

7世、8世回王墓室内景
The interior of the coffin chambers of the 7th and 8th Uygur Kings

处于陵园中心位置的高大建筑物，是第七世回王伯锡尔的陵墓。陵墓高17.8米，东西长20米，南北宽15米。陵墓下部为长方形，上部由墙垣支撑着巨大的穹窿顶。圆形拱顶外镶绿色琉璃砖，顶部为葫芦形，上悬弯月。下部四周外墙，镶砌着蓝色祥云白底琉璃砖，和绿色祥云琉璃砖，构筑成美丽的图案。上圆下方的造型，蓝绿相间的琉璃砖，使得王陵鲜艳夺目，流光溢彩。陵墓四角，有高大的塔柱，尖拱式门坐东面西，墓门两侧的塔柱，中间空心，筑有36级台阶，盘旋而上可达墓顶。穹窿顶四周为平台，登上平台可眺望四野，田园村庄尽收眼底。陵墓内部墙面，一片粉白，间有蓝色祥云花团，色调简洁素雅，华美庄重。

The largest building in the center of the tomb complex is the tomb of the seventh Uygur King Bosir. The tomb is 17.8 meters high, 20 meters long from east to west and 15 meters wide from south to north. Built on a rectangle base, the tomb is enveloped by a huge vault that is supported by the walls. The exterior of the vault is covered with green glazed bricks. The top of the vault is a gourd shaped sign hanging with a crescent moon. Beautiful patterns decorate the outside of the walls with white glazed bricks with blue auspicious clouds as well as green glazed bricks with auspicious clouds. The shape of the rectangle base and round arch top and the color of blue and green glazed bricks make the tomb bright. There are lofty pillars on the four corners of the tomb. The pointed arch faces the west and the pillars on both side of the arch are hollow. It has a spiral flight of stairs with 36 steps leading to the top of the tomb. Around the top is a flat roof. Step on it, and the vast expanse of open ground and gardens and villages comes into view. Entering the tomb, the style is simple and elegant, with the white walls painted with blue floral patterns of auspicious clouds.

整个陵墓是典型的伊斯兰风格，外观庄严雄伟，与蓝天白云映衬成景，堪称伊斯兰陵墓建筑艺术一大杰作。

哈密回王墓中别具特色的建筑，将多种建筑风格融汇于一体，既是当时各族工匠们的智慧结晶，也是中国多民族文化相互影响相互融合的历史见证，更是民族团结的象征。

2006年5月被国务院公布为第六批全国重点文物保护单位。

The mausoleums of Uygur Royal Family are the typical Islamic style. With the solemn and grand appearance, the mausoleums, against the azure sky and clouds, are a masterpiece among the architectures of Islamic mausoleums.

As distinctive buildings, the mausoleums of the Uygur Royal Family absorb various architectural styles. The mausoleums are great intellectual achievements of multi-national craftsmen, as well as historical witness to the multi-national interaction and harmony of cultures, and a symbol of national unity.

In May 2006, the Mausoleums of the Uygur Royal Family were designated by the State Council in the sixth group of Key Cultural Relics under the State-level Protection.

新建的"回王展馆"坐落在清真寺左侧

The new exhibition center of the Uygur Kings is situated to the left side of the Mosque

坐落在东山深处的回王夏宫"庙尔沟夏宫"

Miaoergo Summer Palace, the summer palace of the Uygur Kings, is situated in the mountains to the East

王爷府
The king′s palace

回王府

回王府俗称“王爷台”，位于哈密回城北靠西门处。王府初建于明永乐年间（1403–1424），当时为蒙古王府。哈密回王始祖额贝都拉于1697年协助清政府平定噶尔丹叛乱后受到康熙皇帝的封赏，他从内地请来汉族工匠，兴建回王府，清康熙四十五年（1706）落成。后经几代回王扩建，至七世回王伯锡尔时，已建成为一座融合中原和伊斯兰建筑艺术的规模宏大的府第。同治六年（1867）哈密起义军攻进回城，王府大部被毁。光绪八年（1882），九世回王沙木胡索特袭王位后，重新修复、扩建了回王府。王府占地百余亩，大花园、莲花池占地百余亩，房屋800余间。整个府第重门堂舍，亭榭园林，朱漆红柱，飞檐起脊，奇花异草，果木成荫，融合了汉、维、满、蒙等多种建筑风格，是民族多元文化的完美体现与和谐统一。王府不幸于1931年当地农民暴动中被毁，连一点残垣断壁都没有留下。

The Mansion of Uygur Kings

Lying at the west gate in the north of Huicheng Township, Hami City, the mansion of Uygur Kings, also called Wangyetai, was first built during the reign (1403-1424) of the Ming Emperor Yongle and served as the Mongolian King's mansion. In 1697, by helping the Qing government suppress the Geerdan rebellion, the first Uygur King Erbeidula was rewarded by Emperor Kangxi. And then Erbeidula invited the craftsmen of the Han ethic group from inland to build a mansion for him in Hami. It was completed in 1706, the 45th year of the Qing Emperor Kangxi and was enlarged by the subsequent Uygur Kings. By the reign of the seventh Uygur King Bosir, it had been built into a giant mansion, blending the Islamic and Central Plain styles of architecture. In 1867, the sixth year of the Emperor Tongzhi, during an uprising by the army of Hami Huicheng was attacked and the most of the mansion was destroyed. In 1882, the eighth year of the Emperor Guangxu, the ninth Uygur King Samohosot succeeded and rebuilt and enlarged the mansion. The mansion covers an area of about seven hectares with more than 800 rooms. Also, a garden and lotus pond occupies the same size area. With the numerous halls and houses, the beautiful gardens with pavilions, the lofty red pillars, the upturned eaves and ridge roll, the rare plants and the shade trees, the mansion adapts the various architectural styles of the Han, Uygur, Man and Mongolian ethnic groups. It is the perfect embodiment of the multi cultural harmony and unity of the ethnic groups. Unfortunately, the original mansion was destroyed in 1931 when a Muslim revolt erupted and nothing was left.

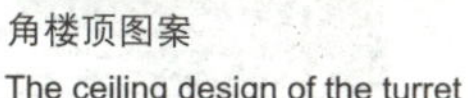

角楼顶图案
The ceiling design of the turret

王爷台门楼一角
A corer of the gate way of the king′s palace

王爷家的四合院
Courtyard of the king's palace

2003年，哈密市人民政府决定重修回王府，并得到了广东省委和政府大力支持，无偿援助1000万元人民币。复原后的回王府占地约13公顷，完全按原貌建造。内部开设宫廷歌舞表演厅、宫廷宴厅、丝绸之路博物馆、哈密历史博物馆、工艺品及纪念品店等旅游服务设施，外部饰以黄土，保持古建筑的原有风格。王爷台上的所有建筑保持不变，回王府的兵营、花园、清真寺、接待厅、马厩等设施基本为原有风格和规模。回王府是民族大团结、大融合的一个永久的象征。它的恢复重建，对于弘扬民族文化，让民族历史文化精髓深人持久延续下去具有现实意义。重建后的回王府将成为哈密市又一张亮丽的旅游名片，它将让你领略到昔日王室贵族的风采和王府风貌。

In 2003, the government of Hami City decided to rebuild the mansion and received 10 million Yuan from the provincial party committee and the government of Guangdong. The refurbished mansion covers an area of 13 hectares with the original appearance. Some tourist service facilities are established inside the mansion such as the show hall for court singing and dancing, the court banquet hall, the museum of the Silk Road, the museum of Hami history, and the research institution of the Uygur Kings history, the arts and crafts shop and the souvenir shop. In addition, loess is paved outside the mansion to keep the original style of ancient architecture. All buildings on the Wangyetai are unchanged. The facilities including barracks, gardens, mosque, reception hall and horse stalls are basically kept in the original style and size. The mansion is an eternal symbol of multi-ethnic national unity and harmony. Its reconstruction is of great practical significance to continue the national development of historical and cultural essences. The refurbished mansion will become a bright tourist attraction for Hami and shows the elegance and beauty of the ancient mansion.

王府的建筑风格，仍然别具一格
The king´s palace has unique style of architecture

王爷台上的角楼属蒙式风格

The turret of the king´s palace is of Mongolian style

王府廊柱

The aisle columns

回王当年的宝座

The ancient throne of the Uygur kings

王爷台全景

The panoramic view of the king´s palace complex

王爷台外景

The exterior of the complex of the king´s palace

回城残留的城墙

Ruins of city walls of Hui City

王府的"点将台"

The Dian Jiang Tai (a tower where the king ever gave out military orders to the officers) of the king´s palace

王府的碉堡
Battlement of the king´s palace

王府的"牌坊"
Memorial archway of the king´s palace

清真寺大门属伊斯兰风格
The main entrance of the mosque is of Islamic style

9世回王的孙子：买合木提·阿不都，目前是农民，也是当地的宗教人士。

The grandson of the 9th Uygur king, Maihemuti·Abudu. He is a farmer as well a local religious representative now

回王地人杰地灵，如今当地的农民画在全国也很有影响

The birth of heroes has brought glory to this place. Now the local farmer paintings are getting popular across the country

原"王府乐队"已成了庞大的群众文化的主体

The original royal band has played a leading role in mass cultural activities now

鼓劲 呐喊加油

Cheering

喀纳斯湖

KANAS LAKE

多彩喀纳斯
Colorful Kanas Lake

喀纳斯湖畔的原始森林风光
Virgin forest by Kanas Lake

喀纳斯湖在中国新疆维吾尔自治区阿勒泰地区布尔津县境内。“喀纳斯”是蒙语“美丽富饶而神秘”的意思，位于阿尔泰山主峰——中、俄、蒙三国边境的友谊峰（海拔4374米）南部中国境内的山地森林带的中部，湖面海拔1374米，湖面长25公里，宽1.6～2.9公里，形如一长豆荚，面积37.7平方公里，约为天山天池的8倍。湖深188.5米，在中国境内湖深仅次于中、朝两国边境的白头山天池（312.7米）。

Kanas Lake is within the territory of Burqin County, Altay Region in Xinjiang Uygur Autonomous Region, China. “Kanas”, a Mongolian word, means “beautiful, richly endowed and mysterious.” It is located in the middle of a mountainous forest south of the Friendship Peak (with the altitude of 4,374 meters), the major peak of the Altai Mountain, on the border of China, Russia and Mongolia. The lake surface is at an altitude of 1,374 meters. The lake is 25 km long and 1.6-2.9 km wide. In the shape of a long bean pod, the lake covers an area of 37.7 square km, about 8 times of that of Tianchi in the Tianshan Mountain. The lake is 188.5 meters deep, second to only Tianchi (312.7 meters) in the Baitoushan Mountain on the border of China and North Korea.

喀纳斯冬景
Kanas Lake in winter

春到喀纳斯
Kanas Lake in spring

喀纳斯湖四周重峦叠嶂，山林犹如画屏。雪岭、青山与绿水浑然一体，湖光山色美不胜收。透过湖边茂密的树林望去，青山烟云缭绕，雪峰倒映碧波。密林深处时而传来马鹿低沉的鸣声。湖边尽是浓密的松、杉、桦、柳和高过人头的草丛，丛林中不时露出狍、鹿的褐黄色身影。成群的野鸭在湖面上嬉戏。大鱼时而跃出水面，激起一片涟漪。湖上风姿兼有南、北方山区湖泊的特色。友谊峰白雪皑皑，犹如一块光洁晶莹的白玉，耸立于群峰之巅。周围的条条冰川，似玉龙飞舞，其中最长的一条，就是长十余公里的喀纳斯冰川，其融水流过丫形的阿克库勒湖，成为喀纳斯的主要补给水源。

Overlapping mountains and peaks encircle Kanas Lake and the landscape of the lake and mountains is beautiful. Looking through the dense forests on the bank of the lake, people can see mist and clouds wind around the green mountains and snow peaks reflecting in the green lake water. Red deer can be found coming from the forest at times. Surrounding the lake are dense pines, firs, birches and willows, as well as brush taller than a man. Dear and roe deer can be seen in the brush every now and then. Groups of wild ducks play on the lake surface. Big fish sometimes jump out of the lake sending ripples across the surface. The scene of the lake has both the southern and the northern characteristics of lakes in mountains. The Friendship Peak with white snow looks like bright and glittering white jade, rising up to the top. The glaciers around it seem like dancing jade dragons and the longest one is the Kanas Glacier which is more than ten kms long. Thawed water from the glacier running across the Akekule Lake in a forked shape is the major water source supplying the Kanas Lake.

喀纳斯湖处于布尔津河上游支流喀纳斯河的中段，夏季湖口流量约50立方米/秒，湖面年变化高差不到30厘米，水量较为稳定，湖岸平缓，湖边的沼生植物生长茂密，整个湖区成为鱼类和水禽产卵繁殖的理想场所。七八月份，在近岸的湖水中，小鱼聚集如云，使湖水为之变色。更有趣的是随着阴晴晨昏，喀纳斯湖水色也有着规律地变化。从山头望去，晴天是深蓝绿色，阴天则是暗灰绿色。夏日晴朗炎热时，湖水又变为微带蓝绿的乳白色，这是由于上游冰川强烈融化，带来大量乳白色粉状冰碛物质所致。有时还会诸色皆备，是有名的“变色湖”。

冬归 Migration in winter

喀纳斯湖 Kanas Lake

The Kanas Lake is in the middle section of the Kanas River, a branch in the upper reaches of the Vurjin River. In summer the flow rate at the mouth of the lake is about 50 cubic meters per second. The depth of the lake varies less than 30 cm during a year. The water volume is comparatively stable and the slope of the bank is gentle. The plants beside the lake grow densely and the whole lake region is an ideal place for fish and water fowl to lay eggs and breed. In July and August small fish will gather near the bank like clouds and make the color of the water change. It is more interesting that the water color of the Kanas Lake will change according to the weather and the time of a day. When seen from the mountain tops, it is deep blue and green on sunny days and dark celadon on cloudy days. In summer on the sunny and hot days the lake water changes to milk white with slight cyan, as the glaciers on the upper reaches thaw quickly and a large amount of milk-white icy slush flows into the lake. Sometimes the lake water will show a variety of colors. It is a well-known “changing-color lake.”

喀纳斯湖水温变化很大，7月中旬正午湖面水温可达20℃以上，适合下水游泳；而傍晚即迅速降温，冰冷刺骨。12月份湖面封冻，喀纳斯湖又像一面白水晶的镜子，当地蒙古族牧民就利用爬犁在湖面运输物资。湖冰要到来年5月才能完全融化。由于湖面强劲谷风的吹送，将上游和倒入湖中的树木吹向湖北端，在这里形成一条百余米宽、两公里长的枯朽浮木带，成为喀纳斯湖一大奇观。每当七八月份，云雾缭绕，群山若隐若现，若在雨后清晨登上湖西哈拉开特山顶，可观赏到喀纳斯云海佛光。

喀纳斯湖码头　The wharf at Kanas Lake

The Kanas Lake water experiences great changes in temperature. In the middle of July at noon the water temperature can reach above 20℃, suitable for swimming, while at nightfall the temperature will decrease quickly and it is ice-cold and nippy. In December the surface freezes over and the Kanas Lake looks like a white crystal mirror and local Mongolian herdsmen make use of sledges to transport materials across the surface of the lake. The lake will not thaw completely until May. Due to waftage by the strong valley wind on the surface, the trees on the upper reaches and those falling down to the lake are blown to the northern end of the lake and form a strip of withered and rotten floating wood of over a hundred meters wide and two kms long. It is a great wonder of the Kanas Lake. In July and August the lake is encircled by mist and clouds and the mountains are only partially visible. When climbing up to the top of Halaket Mountain west of the lake in the morning after rain, people can appreciate a sea of clouds and Buddhist halo.

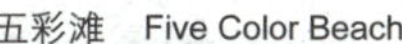

五彩滩　Five Color Beach

喀纳斯湖是第二次大冰期的巨大复合山谷冰川刨蚀而成。当时，喀纳斯冰川长达百余公里，冰川厚度300米以上。由于缓慢而稳定的退缩，在喀纳斯湖口留下了宽约1公里、高50～70米的冰碛垄，而后即迅速退缩，形成了现在喀纳斯湖的基础。现代冰川和古冰川地貌的发育、保存都相当完好。至今在湖东岸的高陡崖边，还保存着几十米长、布满丁字形冰川擦痕的羊背石。有趣的是在这羊背石上，还有古代岩石壁画，给喀纳斯增添了历史人文景观。那冰碛垄便成了当地举行阿肯弹唱会和赛马的好场所。

这里年降雨量700～800毫米。由于山体高差很大，垂直自然景观带非常明显，在湖边就可饱览阿尔泰山7个自然景观带，层次鲜明，各呈异彩。它们自下而上分别是黑钙土草甸草原带、山地灰黑土针、阔叶林带、山地漂灰土针叶林带、亚高山草甸带、高山草甸带、冰沼土带和永久冰雪带。从山下到山顶，具备了从温带草原至极地苔原冰雪地带的多种自然景观，因此，也为多种类型动植物的生存创造了条件。

喀纳斯冬

Kanas in winter

The Kanas Lake was formed during the second grand ice age from peeled glaciers of huge compound valleys. At that time the Kanas Glacier was more than a hundred kms long and over 300 meters deep. Due to slow and stable shrinking, a moraine ridge of about 1 km wide and 50 to 70 meters high was left at the mouth of the Kanas Lake. Later due to fast shrinking, the foundation for the present Kanas Lake was formed. The modern glaciers and ancient glacier relief are considerably intact. Today beside the abrupt cliff on the eastern bank of the lake on the roche Moutonnee with there are scores of meters of area covered with fork-shaped scrapes made by the glaciers. It is interesting that on the roche Moutonnee there is an ancient rock painting which adds a historical human touch to Kanas. That moraine ridge serves as a good place to hold Akeng singing and concerts and horse racing.

赛马 Horse racing

The annual rainfall is 700-800 mm. Due to greatly varying mountains heights there are distinct vertical scenic zones. On the bank of the lake people can appreciate 7 scenic zones of the Altai Mountain with sharp-cut layers and various colors. The zones include from bottom to top black calcrete meadow and grassland zone, mountainous gray-black earth and coniferous and broadleaf forest zone, mountainous bleached gray earth and coniferous forest zone, sub-alpine meadow zone, alpine meadow zone, ice swamp zone and permanent ice and snow zone. From the foot to the top of mountains, there are several natural scenes from temperate grassland to tundra, which create conditions for various animals and plants to live.

草原石人
Stone statues on the grassland

这一带是中国惟一的南西伯利亚区系动植物分布区，有各种植物近1000种，兽类30多种，鸟类100余种，两栖爬虫类7种，鱼类8种，昆虫300种以上。不同的植物群落层次分明，色彩各异。在25种木本植物中，以挺拔的西伯利亚落叶松、塔形的西伯利亚云杉、苍劲的西伯利亚红松、秀丽的西伯利亚冷杉等为主，构成了湖岸漫山遍野的原始阴暗针叶林带。是中国惟一的欧洲——西伯利亚泰加林系“飞地”。林中枯朽倒木层层叠叠，在朽木及地表枯枝落叶层上长满了苔藓、鹿蹄草、越桔及2～3米高的蔷薇、忍冬等，填塞着20～30米高的、挂满松萝的乔木树冠下的空间，使林内格外阴暗。

在湖边林间空地，则是另一番景色：这里赤芍、柳兰、红花遍地，金莲花、郁金香、水毛茛一片金黄，飞燕草、鸢尾、翠雀花、勿忘我如同蓝色地毯，高大的防风、野胡萝卜的伞形花朵，像是飘在空中的片片白云。它们随季节和生态环境的变化，形成了多姿多彩的花坛，与蓝天、白云、雪峰、碧水及墨绿的森林浑然一体，构成了异常瑰丽的图画。

This region is the only area in China containing animals and plants of the southern Siberian region. There are nearly 1,000 varieties of plants, over 30 kinds of animals, more than 100 kinds of birds, 7 kinds of amphibian reptiles, 8 kinds of fish and over 300 kinds of insects. Different plant groups are distinctive from each other with various colors. The 25 kinds of plants mainly include the tall and straight Siberian larch, pagoda-shaped Siberian spruce, vigorous Siberian red pine, and beautiful Siberian fir which compose the primitive dark coniferous forest zone all over the mountains near the banks of the lake. It is the only European-Siberian "enclave" of boreal forest. In the forests there are layers of withered and rotten trees, and on the rotten trees and the withered branches and leaves on the ground grow moss, wintergreen, bilberry and rosebush and honeysuckle of 2 to 3 meters in height, which fill the space under the crowns of arbors of 20 to 30 meters high which are hung with trailing plants making the forest especially dark.

In the forest beside the lake there is a different scene: there are red peony, and red flowers everywhere, a golden piece of canary-creeper, tulip and water-buttercup, a blue-carpet-like piece of delphinium, fleur-de-lis, and myosotis, and umbrella-shaped flowers of wild carrots which are tall enough to block the wind and look like white clouds in the sky. With the changes of seasons and ecological environment, they form various and colorful parterres and compose an extraordinarily beautiful picture with blue sky, white clouds, snow peaks, green water and dark green forest as one integrated mass.

草原盛会
Celebration on the grassland

喀纳斯是野生动物的乐园，也是中国新疆维吾尔自治区鸟兽种类最多的地区，在密密的原始森林和遍生的鲜花草甸中还栖息着众多受国家保护的珍禽异兽。湖中哲罗鲑(大红鱼)、红鳞鲑（小红鱼）、北极回鱼和江鳕等冷水鱼成群结队，游来游去。红鱼最大的可长达4米、重数十公斤，可一口吞下一只野鸭。

以喀纳斯湖为中心，现已建立了自然景观保护区，总面积达10030平方公里。奇、特、绝、美的自然景观和浓郁、独特的人文景观，构成了保护区美妙神奇的特色，使其具有很高的科学考察、旅游观光、文化研究的价值。

Kanas is a paradise for wild animals and also the region with the most kinds of animals and birds in Xinjiang Uygur Autonomous Region. In the dense virgin forest and the flowers and meadows all over the mountains there live numerous rare animals that are protected by the state. Groups of cold-water fish such as Hucho taimen (big red fish), red-scale trout (small red fish), north pole fish and codfish swim in the lake. The biggest red fish can be 4 meters long and weighs scores of kg and can swallow a wild duck in one gulp. A natural scenic protection region covering an area of 10,300 square km. has been established with the Kanas Lake as the core. Strange, peculiar, unique and beautiful natural scenes and strong and unique human scenes compose the great and mysterious characteristics of the protection region and make it valuable for scientific investigation, tourism and cultural research.

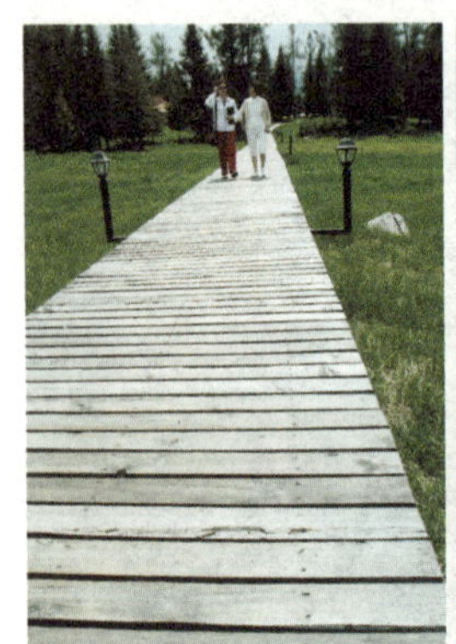

喀纳斯木栈道

Plank road in Kanas

喀纳斯云雾

Clouds over Kanas

卧龙湾

Crunching Dragon Bay

随着季节的不同，喀纳斯湖之美也不尽相同。6月中旬这里绿草芊芊深没人膝，山花烂漫，硕大的野生赤芍药与橘黄色的金莲花漫山遍野地展露芬芳，犹如百花园，林间各种鸟儿婉转啼鸣，蝴蝶时而翩翩起舞，时而短暂停落，好一派青翠欲滴的绿色世界。

秋天是喀纳斯最美的季节，仿佛是魔术师把金灿灿的白桦树、落叶松，红艳艳的野刺梅、哈熊果与苍翠的云杉交织成一个色彩缤纷的调色板，墨绿清澈的湖水将蓝天、白云、飞鹰、峰峦、林影映入其中，一时江山如画，令人沉醉。多少文人墨客作赋吟诗，抒发赞美之情。元代（1206–1368）政治家、诗人耶律楚材有诗赞道：“谁知西域逢佳境，始信东君不世情。图沼方池三百所，澄澄春水一池平。”

秋 Autumn

秋魂 Kanas in autumn

山花 Mountain flowers

秋色初染白桦树 Birch in the early of autumn

With the change of seasons the Kanas Lake displays different beauties. In the middle of June the green grass is lush and knee-high. Flowers are brilliant on the mountains, and huge wild red peonies and orange canary-creepers exude their fragrance all over the mountains. It is like a hundred-flower garden. In the forest birds sing sweetly and butterflies dance. It is a green and lush world.

Autumn is the most beautiful season in Kanas. Like a magician, it interweaves the golden silver birches and conifer trees, brightly red wild calyx canthus and green spruces in a colorful palette. The dark green and clear lake water reflects blue sky, white clouds, flying eagles, mountains and peaks and forests. It is an intoxicating picture. Many literati and scholars composed poems to express their admiration. Yelu Chucai, a politician and poet of the Yuan Dynasty (1206-1368), wrote a poem to praise the scene, “who knows there is a beautiful scene in the Western Region, and I began to believe the outstanding emotion of the eastern monarch. There are three hundred various ponds and a lake is full of clear spring water.”

冬日踏雪 Travel in the snow in winter

In winter Kanas is immersed in a vast expanse of white snow and ice and everything is covered in snowflakes. All the trees without leaves are covered with silver threads, the tall and straight pines and firs are hung with fluffy and heavy snowflakes, and the hardy silver birches wear caps of ice and snow, but are still strong and straight in a heroic posture. They seem to make people see that the ice and snow bound severe winter contains the inside information of intelligence and life. The quiet white and the lonely sledges slowly crossing the snowfield compose the most classic scene in this world of ice and snow.

冬季的喀纳斯是个粉妆玉砌的世界，山川、河流、树木、房屋……全都沉浸在白茫茫的冰雪中。落光叶子的树木，一律改扮成满头银发，挺拔的松杉上则挂满了蓬松松、沉甸甸的雪花，耐寒的白桦树虽然也戴上了冰雪帽子，但仍旧不减其雄姿，坚强挺立着，仿佛要让人们看到这冰封雪锁的严冬饱藏着智慧和生命的底蕴。寂静的白色和雪原上踽踽独行的爬犁，构成这个冰雪世界最经典的景象。

雪后月亮湾 The Moon Bay after snow

喀纳斯湖及其周边的主要景点有：

卧龙湾　这是进入喀纳斯景区后第一个要停留的地点。河面宽阔成湖，湖中部有一个形状别致的小岛，远看酷似一条剑龙，尾巴高高翘起，眠卧在湖中心。

月亮湾　卧龙湾北行1千米，喀纳斯河床形成几个反“S”状河曲，呈半月牙状的河湾被称为“月亮湾”。河湾内有两个酷似脚印的滩岛，当地人称为“神仙脚印”，传说是嫦娥吃了灵药升天时留下的两只脚印；也有人说是当年成吉思汗追赶敌人留下的脚印。

The major scenic spots in the Kanas Lake and the surrounding areas:

Lying Dragon Bay: It is the first stop after entering the scenic region of Kanas. The river is broad and forms a lake. In center of the lake there is an isle in a unique shape. It looks like a stegosaurus from far away, with its tail rising up in the center of the lake.

Moon Bay: One km north of Lying Dragon Bay, the Kanas River forms several bends in the shape of a converse “S”. A river bay in the shape of semi-crescent is called “moon bay”. There are two footprint-shaped isles in the river bay, which are called “god’s footprints” by the local people. According to legends they are two footprints left by Chang’e who ate a panacea and went up to heaven. There is another saying that they are the footprints left by Genghis Khan when chasing an enemy.

卧龙湾初雪

First snow in the Crunching Dragon Bay

传说中成吉思汗在月亮湾留下的两个脚印

The legendary two footprints left by Genghis Khan at the Moon Bay

喀纳斯湖畔的神仙湾 The Immortal Bay in the Kanas Lake

仙境 Fairyland

秋天的神仙湾 The Immortal Bay in autumn

神仙湾 由月亮湾前行3千米，就到神仙湾，这是喀纳斯河一片宽阔的水域，河水异常平缓，若干个小岛组成河心洲，岛上点缀着云杉、白桦和落叶松。微风吹来，碧波荡漾，在阳光的照射下河面闪闪发光，似撒下的一片珍珠，犹如仙界一般，应该是神仙居住的地方——这就是“神仙湾”名字的由来。

Immortal Bay: Marching ahead 3 km from the Moon Bay, people reach the Immortal Bay which is a broad area on the Kanas River. The river water is singularly gentle. There is an islet in the center of the river. The islet is decorated by spruces, silver birches and larches. When a breeze blows the green water ripples. Under the sunshine the river surface glints like scattered pearls. It seems like a fairy land and should be the place where immortals live, hence the name “Immortal Bay”.

天鹅　Swans

鸭泽湖　鸭泽湖位于神仙湾旁一片芦苇浅滩上，是喀纳斯河改道后留下的一片洼地，南端形成一个南北向的宽浅小湖，湖水与周围开阔的沼泽湿地和草原连接，野鸭、大雁和天鹅在宁静的水面上安闲游弋，因此被称作“鸭泽湖”

双湖　双湖距喀纳斯村19千米，喀纳斯湖西岸，呈椭圆形，由2个狭长的小湖串联构成，长1200米，宽约300米，湖水呈无色透明状，远看湖水呈绿色，洁净无污染。双湖处于阿尔泰山南坡森林带，环湖四周云杉、西伯利亚雪松、落叶松、杨树、桦树密布，边缘为茂密的草地，草高为1.5米以上，常有野生动物棕熊、马鹿、野猪等在双湖边出没。湖中多小红鱼，湖水来自恰其阿依特山的冰川消融水和降水，汇聚后注入喀纳斯湖。双湖每年12月结冰，次年5月开始融化。

Duck Pond Lake: It is located in an area of reed shallows, beside the Immortal Bay, left by the Kanas River after it changed its course. In the south a small, broad and shallow lake was formed running south to north. The lake water is connected with the surrounding, broad swamps and grassland. Wild ducks, wild geese and swans prowl leisurely on the tranquil water, hence the name “Duck Pond Lake”.

Twin Lake: It is 19 km from the Kanas Village on the western bank of the Kanas Lake. It is in the shape of an ellipse and composed of two small, long and narrow lakes, 1,200 meters long and about 300 meters wide. The lake water is colorless and transparent, and looks green from far away. It is not polluted. Double Lake is located at the forest zone on the southern slope of the Altai Mountain. Around the lake spruces, Siberian cedars, larches, poplars and birches are densely distributed. At the edge is thick grassland above 1.5 meters high. Wild animals such as brown bears, red deer and wild boars often appear beside the Double Lake. The lake abounds in small red fish. The lake water comes from the thawed water of glaciers from the Chatachi Mountain and rainfall, which gather and run into the Kanas Lake. Twin Lake will freeze in December and begin to thaw in May.

神秘的喀纳斯云海　The mysterious sea of clouds in Kanas

千湖　千湖距喀纳斯村13千米，处于喀拉苏阿仁河和格牙阿能尔库分水岭地带，海拔1800～2000米。千湖，哈萨克语称“六琼库尔”，意思是1000个坑，四周大大小小的湖泊星罗棋布，数以千计。湖泊中最大的黑湖呈马头形，面积1.2平方千米，平均水深5米、其他湖面积均很小，其形状为圆形或长形，分布高度基本一致。湖泊群是古冰川作用的结果。湖泊群周围均为沼泽草地，草高10～15厘米，覆盖率90%。湖水来自冰雪融水和当地降水，均为淡水湖，湖泊群每年12月全部结冰，次年5月解冻。

初春的月亮湾　The Moon Bay in the early spring

Thousand Lakes: It is 13 km from the Kanas Village and located in the watershed between the Kalasu Arin River and Geya Anen Erku. Its altitude is 1,800 to 2,000 meters. Thousand Lakes, called “Liuqiongkur” in the Kazak language, means 1,000 hollows. Around it are dotted thousands of big and small lakes. Of the lakes the biggest one is the Black Lake which is shaped like a horse head. It covers an area of 1.2 square km and the average depth is 5 meters. Other lakes are very small and in circular or oblong shapes and are dispersed in the same way. The lake group is the result of ancient glaciers effects. Around the lake group are swamps and grasslands. The grass is 10 to 15 cm high and the coverage rate is 90 percent. The lake water comes from the thawed water of ice and snow and the local rainfall. They are all fresh-water lakes and will all freeze in December and begin to thaw in May.

中国惟一流入北冰洋的河流额尔齐斯河

The Irtysh River – the only river running to the Arctic Ocean in China

阿克库勒湖 阿克库勒湖位于喀纳斯村东北54千米，从喀纳斯村到阿克库勒湖只有小道。该湖地处别迪尔套山西坡高山带，长6600米，最宽处1900米，面积8.5平方千米，湖面海拔1954米，湖水呈乳白半透明状，外观湖水为白色，略显混浊。主要是上游冰川中的岩块大都为白色花岗岩，经冰川运动，融水把岩石的白色粉末混入冰层内，冰川融化后，融水把岩石的白色粉末带人河流，进人湖泊，使湖水呈白色。阿克库勒湖（哈萨克语，意为“白色湖”）因此而得名。

Akekule Lake: It is 54 northeast of the Kanas Village. There is only a byway from the Kanas Village to the Akekule Lake. The lake is located in the alpine zone on the western slope of the Biedirtao Mountain. It is 6,600 meters long and the widest place is 1,900 meters. It covers an area of 8.5 square km and the altitude of the lake surface is 1,954 meters. The lake water appears milk white and translucent. It is white and a little turbid apparently. The major reason is that the rocks in the glaciers on the upper reaches are mostly white granite. After glacier movement the thawed water brought the white powdered granite to the glaciers. When the glaciers thawed, the water brought the white powder to rivers and lakes, and the lake water appears white, hence the name of “Akekule” (in the Kazak language it means “white lake”).

红叶沟 Red Leaves Valley

喀纳斯晨雾

Morning fog in Kanas

变色湖 喀纳斯湖是有名的“变色湖”一年之中随着不同季节交替。甚至一天之中由晨至夕、天气阴晴，都会有不同的色彩变化，或湛蓝、或碧绿、或黛绿、或灰白，或各色兼备，浓淡参差，在观鱼亭上观看尤为明显。

观鱼亭 建在“骆驼峰”山顶上，与喀纳斯湖湖面的高差有600多米，因处于观察“湖怪”的最佳位置，故名“观鱼亭”。从这里可以看到约3/4的湖面，是景区内能看到湖面面积最大的一个地方。上观鱼亭可以乘汽车从后坡绕上山去，也可以从山前铺设的石阶步行。观鱼亭是喀纳斯游览的必到之地。

冬天的喀纳斯湖 Kanas Lake in winter

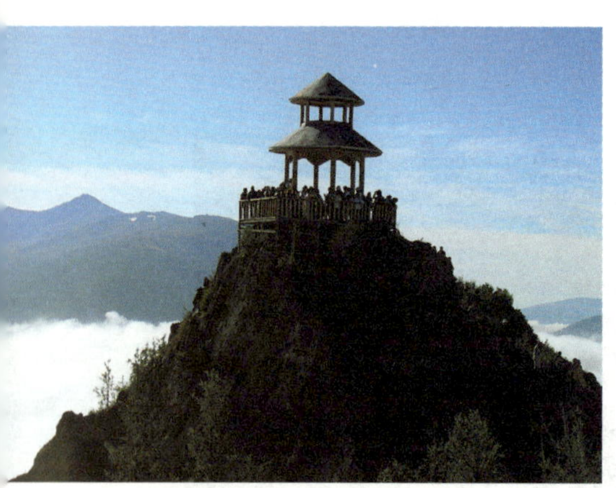

观鱼亭 Observing Fish Pavilion

Color-Changing Lake: Kanas is a famous “color-changing lake” and its color changes with the seasons. It will show different colors from morning to evening or in different weather. It is azure blue, or verdurous, or dark green or grayish white, or several colors at once due to the different depths. The change is obvious especially when viewing from the Observing Fish Pavilion.

Observing Fish Pavilion: It is built on the top of “Camel Peak” and the difference in height between it and the Kanas Lake surface is more than 600 meters. It is the best place to observe “lake monster”, hence the name “Observing Fish Pavilion”. From here people can see about three quarters of the lake, which is the largest view of the lake. Tourists can go up to the mountains by vehicles to the pavilion, or walk up to the pavilion by the stone stairs in front of the mountain. The pavilion is a spot tourists must by all means visit in Kanas .

枯木长堤 喀纳斯山上的树木枯死后，落入湖中。被谷里的风吹送，溯水上移，堆积在喀纳斯湖的北岸尽头处，形成一条长达2000多米的枯木长堤，有1米多高。据说，枯木留恋生养它们的故土，不愿离去，因此没有随波逐流，顺水漂向下游。

吐鲁克岩画 位于喀纳斯湖一道湾的东岸，岩画雕刻在一种特殊的地貌景观——"羊背石" 上面，共有两处。第一处岩画画面大部分模糊不清，只有少许图案可见，如刺猬、野猪、山羊、雪鸡等动物造型；第二岩画图案比较清晰，内容以马、羊、狼、狗、鹿、雪鸡等动物为主，最大的一幅为梅花鹿图案。

Long Withered Wood Dike: The trees on the Kanas Mountain fall down to the lake after becoming withered. Due to the wind in the valley, they will move against the current and pile up at the end of the northern bank of the Kanas Lake to form an over 2,000-meter long withered wood dike that is more than 1 meter high. It is said that the withered wood is reluctant to leave its home, so they do not drift down to the lower reaches.

Turuk Cliff Painting: It is located at the eastern bank of the No.1 bay of the Kanas Lake. The cliff paintings were carved on a special landform, "Roche Mountains". There are two places. In the first place most of the painting is unclear and only a few designs are discernable, such as hedgehog, wild boar, goat and snow chicken. The cliff painting in the second place is comparatively clear and the major designs are animals such as horse, goat, wolf, dog, deer and snow chicken. The largest one is of a spotted deer.

喀纳斯神仙湾牧村

A herdsmen´s village at the Immortal Bay, Kanas

图瓦人家中供奉的成吉思汗像

Genghis Khan portrait consecrated at the household of Tuwa people

晨雾　Morning fog

湖怪　在喀纳斯，没有什么比“湖怪”的传说更有噱头了，据当地的图瓦人传说，喀纳斯湖中有巨大的怪兽，能喷云吐雾，常常吞食岩边的牛羊马匹。这类传说很久以来绵延不断，近年来，更有众多的游客和科考人员宣称亲眼看到长达数十米的黑色物体在湖中漫游甚至兴风作浪，只是缺乏足够的证据证明湖怪的存在。但每隔一段时间，“湖怪”就传得沸沸扬扬、神乎其神，给本已有点过热的喀纳斯旅游吸引来更多的游客。

云海佛光　在喀纳斯谷地云雾遮盖的早上，到上午9～10点左右，太阳升到一定高度时，与太阳相对的方向，会逐渐显现出一个半圆形的彩色光环，赤橙黄绿青蓝紫七色俱备，随着云雾的浓淡，色泽出现深浅明暗的变化，人们称之为“佛光”，前后大约可以持续15分钟左右。随着太阳的升起、光线角度的变化，逐渐隐去。

Lake Monster: In Kanas nothing is more attractive than the story about “lake monster”. According to the legends of local Tuwa people, there is a huge monster in the Kanas Lake, which can spurt out clouds and mist and often swallows the cattle, goats and horses beside the cliff. The legend has persisted for a long time. In recent years numerous tourists and scientific investigators said they had witnessed a black object of scores of meters long swimming and making waves in the lake. But there is lack of evidence to prove the existence of the lake monster. But at regular intervals mysterious stories about “Lake Monster” will spread hot and heavy. It helps attract more tourists to Kanas.

Sea of Clouds and Buddhist Halo: In the morning when the Kanas valley is enveloped by clouds and mist, at around 9 to 10 o’clock when the sun has risen to a certain height a semi-circle colorful halo will appear gradually opposite the sun. It contains seven colors, i.e. red, orange, yellow, green, cyan, blue and purple, and with the changing of the denseness of clouds and mist, the colors will show a different shade, which is called the “Buddhist halo” and usually lasts for about 15 minutes. With the rising of the sun and the changing of the sunlight angle, it will vanish gradually.

佛光
Buddha´s Light

彩虹 喀纳斯地区午后或傍晚的雨后，经常可以看到彩虹，通常是一霓一虹，双双现身。

百花园 百花园坐落在喀纳斯湖西岸，是最为典型的中山森林草甸草原，风景区占地约2.5平方千米，呈缓坡状，宽广开阔，长约3.2千米，宽1.2千米左右。

百花园风景区四面被翠绿的群山所围，每逢夏季，平台绿草似毯，沟间溪流潺潺，满坡的山花，如赤芍、野人球、金钱花、柴胡、金老梅、正梅、正廉、低头葱、独活、白鲜、大黄刺蔷薇、尤花龙胆等，争相怒放，姹紫嫣红，娇艳争辉，清香醉人。百花园因野花茂盛烂漫而得名。

禾木草原 禾木草原距布尔津县城130千米，地处中山森林与山地草甸草原带的交汇区，海拔1124－2300米，地形复杂，山地阴坡森林茂密，苍翠欲滴，有云杉、落叶松、白桦等，马鹿、旱獭、雪鸡等栖息林间；而阳坡绿草满地，繁花似锦。另外还有无与伦比的白色蜂蜜，药用价值极高。该区年降水量达600毫米，水热条件好，植被以禾木科与杂草类为主，主要种类有间茅、毛茛、珠芽蓼、苔草及禾草等，生长期5～9个月，草高20～50厘米、覆盖度90%以上。禾木草原是消夏避暑、休养身心的场所。

Rainbow: In the Kanas region after rain in the afternoon or at nightfall, a rainbow is often visible. And usually a secondary rainbow would also appear.

Hundred-Flower Garden: It is located at the western bank of the Kanas Lake and is the most representative middling mountain forest and meadow grassland. The scenic spot covers an area of 2.5 square km on a gentle slope. It is wide and open and is about 3.2 km long and 1.2 km wide.

The Hundred-Flower Garden scenic region is surrounded by lush mountains. In summer the green grass on the platform seems like carpet, rivulets in the valley flow slowly, and the very beautiful mountain flowers all over the slope are in full

禾木村 Hemu Village

bloom, fragrant and intoxicating, such as red peony others. The Hundred-Flower Garden got its name from the flourishing and brilliant wild flowers.

Hemu Grassland: It is 130 km from the downtown of Vurjin County and located at a place where middling mountain forests and the mountainous meadow grassland meet. With an altitude of 1,124 to 2,300 meters, it is complex landform. On the northern slope of the mountain, the forests are dense and lush, including spruce, larch and silver birch, and red deer, marmot and snow chicken live in the forest. The southern slope of the mountain is covered in grass and beautiful flowers. In addition there is an incomparable white honey with a very high medicinal value. In the region the annual rainfall reaches 600 mm. The plants are mostly cereal crops and rank grass, such as cuckoo-bud, moss and grass. Their growth period is from 5 to 9 months, the grass is 20 to 50 cm high and the coverage rate is above 90 percent. Hemu Grassland is a site suitable for summer holidays and recreation.

漂流　Drifting

海流滩草原　海流滩草原坐落于布尔津县窝依莫克乡境内，四面环山，盆地内地势平坦，多溪流支沟，面积147.3平方千米，生长着低矮的牧草，植被有禾草、苔草、早熟禾、大针茅、羊茅等，杂草类有野豌豆、萤花、黄花苜蓿、野蔷薇等，草高一般在10～20厘米，覆盖度70%左右，主要生长期5～9月。每年夏秋之际，整个盆地浅草平铺，牛羊成群，白色的毡房星星点点散布其中，蓝天与绿色草原融为一体，一派宽阔坦荡的草原风光。

海流滩草原西北边缘的山地阴坡，生长着茂密的云杉林。从山地四周流入盆地涓涓溪流，荡入盆地中央，形成片片沼泽草地。盆地内夏季凉爽，为优良的避暑胜地。

Hailiutan Grassland: It is located within the territory of Oyimuk Township, Vurjin County and is encircled by mountains. In the basin the landform is flat and there are many rivulets and branch gullies. It covers an area of 147.3 square km. Low forage grasses grow there. The vegetation includes grass, moss and precious grain. The grasses include wild pea, yellow-flower alfalfa and wild rosebush. The grass is 10 to 20 cm high, the coverage rate is about 70 percent and the growth period is from May to September. In summer and autumn the whole basin is covered by shallow grasses, and there are flocks and herds and white yurts scattered about. The blue sky and the green grassland integrate and a broad and level grassland scene comes into view.

On the northern slope of the northwestern edge of Hailiutan Grassland grows a thick spruce forest. Rivulets run from mountains to the basin and form areas of swamp grasslands. In the basin it is cool in summer and it is a good place for passing summer holidays.

湖边图瓦人的毡房
The Tuwa People's yurt by the Lake

喀纳斯图瓦人木屋
Tuwa people's cottage in Kanas

喀纳斯的图瓦人 在喀纳斯生活着一些神秘的图瓦人。图瓦人在隋唐（581–907）时称“都播”，元代（1206–1368）称图巴或乌梁海人。按中国目前的民族划分，属于蒙古族的支系。

目前，喀纳斯村和邻近的禾木村、白哈巴村共居住着2000多图瓦人，他们使用的图瓦语，是中国现存的稀有语种，隶属于阿勒泰语系突厥语族。

图瓦人久居山林地带，以放牧和狩猎为生，又被称作“林中百姓”，也有人称其为“云间部落”。由于过去他们极少与外界联系，因此比较完整地保存了其古老的部落氏族观念和宗教信仰，在许多地方都留下了岩刻、岩画、祭祀和墓葬等丰富的历史文化遗迹。

图瓦人有3个比较大的节日，分别是春节、敖包节和邹鲁节。图瓦人也像汉族人一样欢度春节，只是他们欢庆春节的方式有所不同。每当大雪封山，湖面结冰，春节来临时，图瓦人就身着节日盛装，欢聚在喀纳斯湖面上举行赛马、射箭、摔跤、滑雪橇等比赛，然后举行全村人的酒会，并在喇嘛的诵经声中欢度春节。

弹唱的图瓦人
Tuwa people are playing and singing

Tuwa People in Kanas: Some mysterious Tuwa people live in Kanas. Tuwa people were called “Dubo” in the Sui and Tang Dynasties (581-907) and “Tuba” or “Wulianghai” people in the Yuan Dynasty (1206-1368). In accordance with the division of ethnic groups in China at present, they belong to a branch of the Mongolian ethnic group.

At present more than 2,000 Tuwa people living in Kanas Village and nearby Hemu Village and Baihaba Village. They speak in the Tuwa language which is a rare language existent in China and belongs to the Turkish language branch of the Altay language family.

Tuwa people have lived in forests for a long time and mainly depend on herding and hunting. They are also called “common people in forests” and “tribes in clouds”. As they lacked contact with outside world in the past, they have reserved fully their ancient clan concepts and religious belief and left abundant historical and cultural relics such as rock sculpture, rock painting, offering sacrifice and graves.

Tuwa people have three grand festivals, i.e. the Spring Festival, Obo Festival and Zoulu Festival. Tuwa people spend the spring festival joyfully like the Han people, except for their different ways of spending the festival. When mountain passes are closed by snow, the lake surface is frozen and the spring festival is coming, Tuwa people will dress up for the festival, gather on the surface of the Kanas Lake, hold games such as horseracing, archery, wrestling and skiing, and then hold a wine party for the whole village while listening the sound of lamas reading sutras.

图瓦老人额尔德西生前吹楚吾儿
A late Tuwa named Erdersi was blowing Chuwuer

哈萨克族小女孩
A Kazak little girl

喀纳斯湖边的篝火晚会
Camp fire party by the Kanas Lake

哈萨克族牧民 Kazak herdsmen

做奶酒 Making milk wine

敖包节又称“塔克恩”节，这是图瓦人祭祀天地日月和大自然的节日，每年都在春暖花开的6月举行。他们将过节的地点选在水草丰美的高山丘陵，各家各户都携儿带女并各自带上一道拿手的好菜或上好的食品，团聚在中间植有被尊为“神树”的敖包周围，焚香点烛，每人往树上绑一根布条（布条以白色为主），再抱一块石头堆加在敖包上，然后各自拿着从家中带来的食品，由年长者带领绕着敖包一边念经唱歌，一边不断向上撒着食品（此时妇女不能参加）。绕完3圈后，参加者不分老少都要向敖包跪拜磕头，祈求上天降福于人间，祈求风调雨顺，牲畜兴旺。礼毕，开始进行赛马、摔跤、射箭等蒙古族传统的民间体育、娱乐活动，并宰羊煮肉、载歌载舞，然后全村男女老少围坐在一起，吃烤肉、喝奶酒，共同欢度节日。

邹鲁节即 “点灯节”，又称入冬节，时间是每年的农历十月二十五日，这也是喀纳斯湖畔图瓦人的特有节日。在这一天，整个夏秋季在外放牧的牧民都要回到村庄，主要是为了纪念活佛马盒卡拉逝世日。

Obo Festival, also called "Tucken", is a festival on which Tuwa people offer sacrifice to heaven, earth, sun, moon and the natural world and is held in June every year during the warmth of spring when all the flowers bloom. They select the high mountains and hills where waterweeds are lush as the place to spend the festival. Every family will bring their children and a good dish they are adept in or some top-grade food, gather around the aobao (heaps of stones used by the Mongolians and Tibetans as markings for roads or boundaries) where a "holy tree" is planted, light joss sticks and candles, tie a list of cloth (mainly white cloth) on the tree for every one, add a stone on the aobao, and, under the supervision of seniors, tossed food into the air while going around the aobao, reading sutras and singing (at this time women are forbidden). After going around it for three circles, all the participants should worship on their knees and kowtow to the aobao, praying to heaven for happiness, good weather for the crops and flourishing livestock. After the ceremony, they will hold the traditional and folk Mongolian sports and entertainment activities such as horseracing, wrestling and archery, kill and cook sheep, sing and dance, and all the villagers sit together to eat roast mutton and drink milk wine, spending the festival happily.

Zoulu Festival, i.e. "festival of lighting", is also called the "festival of winter beginning". It is on the 25th day of the lunar tenth month every year. It is a particular festival owned by the Tuwa people on the bank of the Kanas Lake. On that day all the herders who have gone out for herding in summer and autumn will come back to villages to commemorate the day when Living Buddha Mahakala passed away.

敖包　Cairns

夏天的喀纳斯游人如织

Many people visit Kanas in summer time

禾木之晨
Morning in Hemu Village

驼影
Camels

盘羊 Argali

Animals and Plants: With the mention of Kanas scenic region, there are many aspects of uniqueness: it is the unique natural protection region in China which borders on four states (China, Russia, Mongolia and Kazakhstan), and the source of the unique Arctic Ocean water system, the largest branch Vurjin River of the Orchis River. The Kanas Lake is also the unique region with the distribution of Southern Siberian animals and plants in China. There are precious trees belonging to Siberian family, such as larch, red pine, spruce, and fir, as well as many birch forests. Animals, birds, amphibian, fish and insects live there.

The Kanas Lake is a god-given region in China which has a European ecological system. In the protection region there are 798 kinds of plants including 30 kinds of rare plants, 39 kinds of animals, 117 kinds of birds and 7 kinds of fish, including 5 kinds of the first-grade state protection animals and 13 kinds of the second-grade state protection animals, in addition to 9 kinds of other rare animals and no less than 60 new species of insects and fungus.

动植物 提到喀纳斯景区，就要提到它的很多惟一：这里是中国惟一四国（中国、俄罗斯、蒙古、哈萨克斯坦）接壤的自然保护区，是中国惟一的北冰洋水系——额尔齐斯河最大支流布尔津河的发源地。喀纳斯湖还是中国惟一的南西伯利亚区系动植物分布区，生长有西伯利亚区系的落叶松、红松、云杉、冷杉等珍贵树种和众多的桦树林。兽类、鸟类、两栖爬行类动物，以及鱼类、昆虫类在此繁衍生息，更是生趣无限。

喀纳斯湖是中国极其难得具有欧洲生态系统的区域，保护区内有植物798种，其中珍稀植物30种，动物39种，国家一级保护动物5种，二级13种，其它稀有动物9种，鸟类117种，鱼类7种，昆虫真菌的新种记录不少于60个。

转场 Transhumance

巴音布鲁克草原

BAYINBULAK GRASSLAND

水草丰美的巴音布鲁克草原

Bayinbulak Grassland, a place with plenty of water and lush grass

美丽的巴音布鲁克草原，位于天山南麓，巴音郭楞蒙古自治州和静县西北，大小尤尔都斯盆地中。

Lying in the grand and lesser Yurdos Basin, the Bayinbulak Grassland is situated on the south side of Tianshan Mountain in northwestern HeJing County, in the Bayingolin Mongolian Autonomous Prefecture.

巴音布鲁克草原的蒙古包

Mongolian yurts on the Bayinbulak Grassland

巴音布鲁克草原上放牧

Grazing on the Bayinbulak Grassland

海拔2000－2800米的巴音布鲁克草原风景如画
Picturesque scenery at the altitude of 2,000 to 2,8000 meters in the Bayinbulak Grassland

巴音布鲁克草原牛羊成群
Flocks and herds on the Bayinbulak Grassland

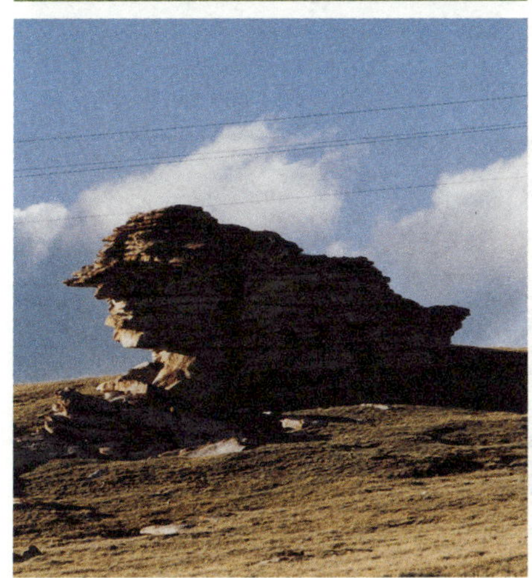

巴音布鲁克草原上的风蚀巨石
A wind-erosion rock on the Bayinbulak Grassland

巴音布鲁克草原

“巴音布鲁克”是蒙古语，意思是“泉水丰富的地方”。巴音布鲁克草原，就是泉水丰富、花草繁茂的大草原。

巴音布鲁克草原的美是辽阔之美。她是我国第二大草原，总面积2.38万平方千米，其载畜量可达250万只。“天苍苍，野茫茫，风吹草地见牛羊”就是巴音布鲁克草原的真实写照。草原上绿草萋萋，花香郁郁，河流如织，飞浪击波，湖泉淙淙充盈四野。

Bayinbulak Grassland

“Bayanbulak” means “place abounding in springs” in the Mongolian language. Just as its name indicates, the grassland is rich in springs and flourishing flowers and grasses.

The Bayanbulak Grassland is the second largest in China. With a total area of 23,800 square km, the vast grassland has a grazing capacity of 2.5 million livestock.

巴音布鲁克草原
The Bayinbulak Grassland

The alpine meadow has mountain chains surrounding it. With elevations varying from 200 to 2,800 meters, the grassland is composed of the Yiky Ordos Basin and the Bakah Ordos Basin. There are 566 mountains and 566 gullies in the grassland, the most famous of which are the Künes Gully, the Bayingolin Gully and the Baluntai Gully. Warm in winter and cool in summer, the gullies are also known as the "green gorges". The Bayanbulak Grassland contains six forest areas, which cover a total area of 22,000 hectares, including famous ones such as the Kunes forest area and the Kurk Wusu forest area. It is very enjoyable to ride across the endless Grassland surrounded by the lofty snow-capped peaks of the Tianshan Mountain.

巴音布鲁克草原的美是山峦之美。巴音布鲁克是高山草场，周围山峦环抱，海拔在200—2800米，由伊克尤尔都斯盆地和巴尕尤尔都斯盆地组成。巴音布鲁克草原上有566道山岭，566条山沟。著名的有巩乃斯沟、巴仑台沟、巴音郭楞沟等。沟内冬季温和，夏季凉爽，素有绿色峡谷之称。巴音布鲁克有大小林区6个，面积2.2万公顷，著名的有巩乃斯林区、奎克乌苏林区。巴音布鲁克大草原尽得山峰之灵秀，山清水秀，山高水长，山林环绕，山静水青。纵马巴音布鲁克大草原，面前是无边无际的绿草地，远方是层林尽染的天山雪峰，令人荡气回肠。

巴音布鲁克草原上的黑鹳
Black stork on the Bayinbulak Grassland

如意湖
Ruyi Lake

巴音布鲁克草原上的九曲十八弯
Jiu Qu Shi Ba Wan (nine bends and eighteen curves) in the Bayinbulak Grassland

巴音布鲁克草原的美是水泽之美。巴音布鲁克草原有大湖泊7个，著名的有天鹅湖、拜尔湖等，小湖泊不计其数。巴音布鲁克有大小泉水13处，著名的有阿尔仙泉、库尔得温泉、哈尔温泉等。巴音布鲁克草原有20条河流纵横交错。著名的有开都河、巩乃斯河、阿拉沟河、巴音郭楞河等。巴音郭楞人民的母亲河孔雀河在巴音布鲁克大草原蜿蜒盘旋，游来荡去，尽情玩耍之后，才冲击峡谷，流进博斯腾湖。

巴音布鲁克草原的美是花草之美。这里是花草大世界，百花争荣，千草竞绿。

The Bayanbulak Grassland has seven big lakes such as the Swan Lake and the Ber Lake, etc as well countless smaller lakes. There are 13 springs including the Arsin spring, Kurd hot spring and the Har hot spring. Twenty rivers crisscross the grassland, including the Kaiduhe River, Kunnes River, Alagou River, and Bayingolin River. The Kongquehe (Peacock) River, the mother river for people living in Bayingolin, swings across the grassland before emptying into the Bostan Lake.

The Bayanbulak Grassland is richly endowed with a variety of flowers and lush grasses.

巴音布鲁克草原上的滩羊
Tan sheep on the Bayinbulak Grassland

巴音布鲁克草原的美还是物产之美。这里幅员辽阔，地势平坦，水草丰美，遍地皆是优质的“酥油草”。这里盛产被誉为“草原四宝”的焉耆马、巴音布鲁克大尾羊、中国的美利奴羊和有“高原坦克”之称的牦牛，被誉为“草原四宝”。

With plenty of water and grasses, especially the desirable meadow fescue, the grassland abounds in the “four measures of the grassland”: the Yanqi horse, the Bayanbulak fat-tailed sheep, the Chinese Merino sheep and the yak.

牧民子弟学校
School for herdsman´ s children

巴音布鲁克天鹅湖风光
The Swan Lake on the Bayinbulak Grassland

巴音布鲁克天鹅湖上优雅的天鹅
Elegant swans on the Swan Lake of Bayinbulak

天鹅湖

巴音布鲁克草原上有一片总面积达1370多平方千米的湖沼星罗棋布的水域，是中国最大的天鹅繁殖、栖息地，它就是巴音布鲁克天鹅湖。

天鹅湖由河溪（河流）、湖泊、沼泽草地组成，天鹅湖区生活着大天鹅、小天鹅、疣鼻天鹅以及禿鹫、灰雁等各种鸟类共计128种，数量则达数十万只，是一个名副其实的“鸟类天堂”。大天鹅在天鹅湖分布数量最多，有近1万只。

Swan Lake

The rivers, lakes and swamps scattered throughout the Bayanbulak Grassland combine to form a water area covering over 1,370 square km. which is known as the Swan Lake because it is the largest swan habitat in China. Know as the “paradise for birds”, the Swan Lake is home to 128 species of birds, such as the whooper swan, whistling swan, mute swan, condor, and grey-leg goose, amounting to some 100,000 birds. The whooper swan is the most numerous, totaling around 10,000.

蓑羽鹤
Demoiselle Crane

天鹅湖白天鹅
White swans on the Swan Lake

成群的天鹅在悠闲地觅食
Flocks of swans are looking for food casually

天鹅湖 The Swan Lake

每年3—4月，以大天鹅、小天鹅和疣鼻天鹅为主的一万多只珍禽都会成群结队飞过崇山峻岭，来到天鹅湖繁衍生息，至10—11月再迁离，居留期长达半年以上。

巴音布鲁克为什么能吸引众多的天鹅和珍禽来此栖息？原来天鹅湖有得天独厚的地理环境和爱鸟如子的当地居民的保护。

During March and April each year, tens of thousands of rare birds including the whooper swan, whistling swan, and mute swan fly over towering mountains and migrate to the Swan Lake. They live here for more than half a year before leaving in the period from October to December.

The swans and other rare birds are drawn to Bayinbulak due to the favorable geographical and ecological conditions, as well as the fact that the local people protect and cherish the birds as family members.

天鹅湖之秋
The Swan Lake in autumn

天鹅湖一带，清泉密布，河网交错，水草繁茂，气候凉爽，环境幽静，饵料丰富，这里便成了天鹅、灰鹤、白鹭、斑头雁、金雕、雁鸥、棕尾狂鸟和各种野鸭等众多水禽的乐园。

The numerous lakes, springs and rivers, abundant aquatic plants and insects, as well as the cool climate and quiet environment make the Swan Lake the ideal resting and breeding place for the birds.

巴音布鲁克天鹅湖天鹅与羊群和睦相处
Live in harmony- the flock of sheep and swans on the Swan Lake of Bayinbulak

天鹅 Swans

天鹅湖之冬 The Swan Lake in winter

巴音布鲁克草原人烟稀少，当地蒙古族牧民视天鹅为天使和幸福鸟，自古以来一直加以精心地保护。有些天鹅得到牧民的精心照顾和喂养，它们早出晚归，犹如家禽：一到深秋，就随大群南迁；次年春，又回到主人家中。

1980年，巴音布鲁克天鹅保护区建立，成为全国鸟类环志点（即给鸟类戴上环状科学仪器进行科学考察的中心点）之一，具有重要科研价值，在国际上也具有一定的影响。1986年该保护区被批准为国家级自然保护区。

Regarded by the local people as the birds which bring happiness, the swans have been highly regarded since ancient times. Being carefully attended and fed by local herdsmen, some swans even regard the people as their hosts. When the swans migrate back to Bayinbulak, some of them choose the same houses every year as their home.

In 1980, the Bayinbulak Swan Nature Reserve was established and listed as one of the National Bird Centers of China. The area has since become an important center of scientific research and attracts many visitors from home and abroad. In 1986, the nature reserve was confirmed as one of the state level nature reserves in China.

天鹅　Swans

小天鹅　Cygnets at the Swan Lake

大天鹅　Whooper Swans

巴音布鲁克草原水草丰美
The Bayinbulak Grassland is rich in water and lush grass

雨后巴音布鲁克草原的彩虹
Rainbow over the Bayinbulak Grassland

巴音布鲁克草原上的狐狸
Fox on the Bayinbulak Grassland

巴音布鲁克草原的牛群
Cattle herd on the Bayinbulak Grassland

巴音布鲁克草原上的灰鹤
Common cranes on the Bayinbulak Grassland

草原文化——巴音布鲁克的那达慕盛会

水草丰茂的巴音布鲁克，曾养育过众多的游牧民族。远在2600年前，这里即有姑师人活动。1776年，卫拉特蒙古土尔扈特部17万民众在首领渥巴锡的率领下，从俄国伏尔加河流域举义东归，受到清乾隆皇帝（1711—1799）的热情接待。乾隆遂以富饶辽阔的巴音布鲁克草原，御赐土尔扈特部。几百年来，土尔扈特的后裔们在这里繁衍生息，巴音布鲁克是他们美丽的家乡，神圣的天堂。

Nadam Fair

As early as 2600 year ago, the Bayinbulak was inhabited by the ancient Gushi people (original residents of the Turpan Oasis in today's Xinjiang). In 1776, lead by their leader Wopasi, a group of some 170,000 people of the Wilat Mongol Turhut tribe escaped cruel Russian domination and returned eastward to China from the Volga River. They were settled in the fertile Bayinbuak Grassland by the Emperor Qianlong of the Qing Dynasty (1711—1799). The Turhut people have been living here for generations, loving the grassland as their dear home and sacred heaven.

高山兀鹫　Gyps himalayensis

巴音布鲁克草原养育着肥美的羊群　Thriving flocks of sheep on the Bayinbulak Grassland

兀鹫　Vultures

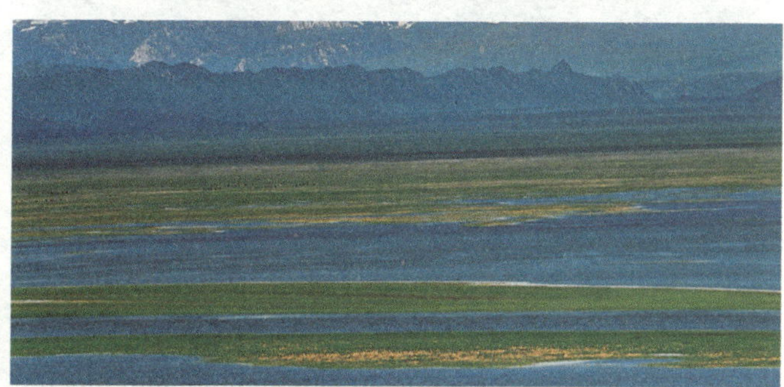

天山下的巴音布鲁克湿地　Wetland in Bayinbulak at the foot of Tianshan Mountain

巴音布鲁克草原晚霞　Sunset glow over the Bayinbulak Grassland

夕阳余辉　Sunset afterglow

巴音布鲁克草原奔驰的骏马

Horses are galloping on the Bayinbulak Grassland

In commemoration of the returning, local people hold the annual Nadam Fair from the fourth to the sixth day of the sixth month of the lunar year. On these days, people will dress up and get together to celebrate their most grand festival. The fair originated from the traditional festival of the Turhut people, the Taglen Festival. The Taglen Festival is the festival for paying sacrifices to Aobao (a pile of stones, earth and grass used by Mongolians as a road sign or boundary sign and in the old days was regarded as the dwelling place of a god where sacrifices were offered). People will hang colorful prayer flags on the branches of the Aobao and chant to pray for peace, a plentiful harvest and happy year. There are other activities such as horse racing, archery contests, and commerce and so on during the Nadam Fair.

草原的精灵——旱獭

Marmot- sprite on the grassland

为纪念东归，每逢农历六月初四至初六，人们都要身穿盛装，从四面八方聚集到巴音布鲁克草原上，参加一年一度的草原那达慕艺术节。那达慕艺术节是巴音布鲁克的盛典，源自土尔扈特的传统节日——塔格楞节。“塔格楞”是土尔扈特部蒙古族祭祀祈福的“敖包”，“塔格楞节”就是祭敖包节。届时，土尔扈特人就会带上经幡，把各种不同颜色的布条挂在“塔格楞”的树条上，诵经朝拜，以求山川宁静、人畜两旺、幸福安康。那达慕艺术节上还要进行赛马、射箭等文化活动和商品交流，让人目不暇接，留恋忘返。

中国新疆名胜古迹 PLACES OF HISTORIC INTEREST AND SCENIC BEAUTY IN XINJIANG, CHINA
阿尔金山自然保护区
ARJIN MOUNTAIN NATURE RESERVE
阿勒泰市
塔城市
克拉玛依市
博乐市
伊宁市
昌吉市
乌鲁木齐市
吐鲁番市
哈密市
库尔勒市
阿克苏市
阿图什市
喀什市
阿尔金山自然保护区
和田市

巍峨苍茫的阿尔金山山脉
The giant Arjin Mountain range

藏野驴
Tibetan wild donkey (Equus kiang)

阿尔金山自然保护区位于阿尔金山南部东昆仑山北部，西起若羌和且末两县分界线，东接青海，南临西藏，东西长360公里，南北宽190公里，总面积4.5万平方公里，是目前中国最大的综合性自然保护区。

The Arjin Mountain Nature Reserve lies between the southern part of the Arjin Mountain range and the northern part of East Kunlun Mountain range. It extends 360 km from Qinghai Province in the east to the boundary between Ruoqiang County and Qiemo County in the west. With the Tibet Autonomous Region to its south, the nature reserve measures 190 km from north to south. The Arjin Mountain Nature Reserve covers a total area of 45,000 square km, thus it is recognized as the largest comprehensive nature reserve in China.

保护区为高山环绕的封闭性盆地，四周高山海拔均在5000米以上，其平均海拔4500米，有野生植物241种，野生动物现已发现60多种。其中国家一类保护动物有野牦牛（约1万多头）、藏野驴（3万多头）、藏羚羊（9万余只）、雪豹、盘羊、藏雪鸡、黑颈鹤等7种，二类保护动物11种，三类保护动物4种。矿藏资源有玉石、水晶、云母、铁、锌、天然碱等14种，尤以玉石、黄金和石棉最为有名。保护区保留了较完整而原始的生态系统，具有极大的科研价值。区内著名的魔鬼谷、阴阳湖等景点更为保护区增添了神秘色彩和迷人的魅力。

With an average elevation of 4,500 meters, the nature reserve is a basin surrounded by great mountains rising more than 5,000 meters above sea level. It is now home to 241 species of wild plants and some 60 species of wild animals. Seven species of wild animals are now under first class State protection, including some 10,000 wild yaks, some 30,000 Tibetan wild donkeys, some 90,000 Tibetan antelopes, and a large number of snow leopards, argalis, Tibetan snowcocks and black-necked cranes. Furthermore, there are 11 species of animals under second class State protection and four species under third class State protection. The nature reserve is richly endowed with mineral resources, with abundant reserves of jade, crystal, mica, iron, zinc, trona and eight other minerals. Of them, jade, gold and asbestos are the most precious ones. The ecological system of the nature reserve has remained intact over the passage time, offering scientists an excellent place to do research. The Moguigu Valley (Devil's Valley) and the Lake of Yin and Yang (Whale Lake) are the two most famous sites in the nature reserve. Their stunning landscapes make the place mysterious and enchanting to outsiders.

阿尔金山自然保护区的地形地貌

The topography and geomorphology of the Arjin Mountain Nature Reserve

阿尔金山生态环境

The Ecological environment of the Arjin Mountain

冰川　The Glacier

阿尔金山

阿尔金山西起且末河上游，东至当金山口与祁连山相接，长约270公里，最宽处100公里，是塔里木盆地和柴达木盆地的分界山。山势西高东低，山脊线3500～4000米，最高峰尤苏巴勒，海拔6161米，位于若羌县城东南。阿尔金山，《汉书》中称为“南山”，唐玄奘去天竺求经时曾由此山穿过。这里雨量稀少，气候干燥，整个山地以荒漠植被为主，完整地保留了原始高原生态环境。全国最大的自然保护区——阿尔金山自然保护区，以及阿尔金山野骆驼保护区，就坐落在若羌县境内的阿尔金山上。在保护区内，栖息着数以万计的藏野驴、藏羚羊、野牦牛、野骆驼、黑颈鹤等国家一类保护动物，再加上奇特的高山沙漠、数十个高山湖泊、原始的自然景观，具有很高的科学考察和探险旅游价值。据新闻媒介报道，近几年还在阿尔金山发现了雪人的踪迹，这更为人迹罕至的阿尔金山蒙上了一层神秘的色彩。

Arjin Mountain

The Arjin Mountain extend 270 km from the Qiemo River in the west to the Dangjin Pass of the Qilian Mountains in the east. The widest part measures 100 km. As the demarcation line of Tarim Basin and Qaidam Basin, the mountain range is higher in the west and lower in the east. The zigzagging mountain ridge extends about 3,500 to 4,000 meters long. With an elevation of 6,161 meters, the highest peak, Yusubale, is located in the southeastern part of Ruoqiang County. According to the *Book of Han*, a classic Chinese historical writing on the history of the Western Han Dynasty (206 BC-25 AD), the Arjin Mountains were once called the Nanshan Mountains (the South Mountains). In historical documents of later dynasties, it is recorded that Xuanzang, an eminent monk of the Tang Dynasty (618-907), crossed the mountains when he made his renowned

冰川 The Glacier

到若羌的沙漠公路（老沙漠公路）
The desert highway to Ruoqiang (the old desert highway)

pilgrimage to India. With sparse rainfall and a dry climate, the Arjin Mountain range is mainly covered by desert vegetation. The primitive ecological system on this plateau remains pristine. On the mountain, there are the Arjin Mountain Nature Reserve—the largest one of its kind in China, and the Arjin Mountain Wild Camel Nature Reserve. This area is home to some tens of thousands of wild donkeys, Tibetan antelopes, wild yaks, wild camels, black-necked cranes and other animals under the first class State protection. With special alpine deserts, scores of alpine lakes and a variety of primitive natural landscapes, this area has attracted numerous scientists and adventurous tourists over the years. Recently, traces of a mysterious snowman were reported to have been found in the Arjin Mountain range, drawing another mysterious veil over the uninhabited mountainous area.

阿尔金山的山岩
The rocks in the Arjin Mountain

阿尔金山自然保护区的羊群
The flock in the Arjin Mountains Nature Reserve

阿尔金山自然保护区自然景观优美，这里有世界上海拔最高的积沙滩沙漠、高原内陆不冻湖——阿其克湖、“高原桂林山水”新青峰、冰川密布的木孜塔格冰峰，此外还有千泪泉、阴阳湖、魔鬼谷等景点；在山中还发现了不少用藏文刻写在石头上的密宗咒语。

The nature reserve also boasts a variety of beautiful scenery. Here you can find the world's highest desert—Jishatan Desert, the inland plateau warm-water lake—Lake Achik-kul, the "Guilin on high plateau"—Xinqingfeng, and the ice capped Muztag. In the high mountains perennially enveloped by clouds, there are stone steles inscribed with secret teachings of Tibetan Esoteric Buddhism.

柴达木盆地　The Qaidam Basin

柴达木盆地的风蚀地貌　The wind-erosion landform in the Qaidam Basin

阿尔金山岩溶地貌

阿尔金山岩溶地貌位于阿尔金山自然保护区的阿格山中。岩溶地貌东起布喀达坂山峰，西止阿其克库勒湖，长350公里，宽20～30公里，面积约1万平方公里，深藏在海拔4400～5000米的崇山峻岭之中。

阿尔金山岩溶地貌，是古老的石灰岩经过千百年风吹雨打，溶解分化，造就而成的千姿百态的壮丽景观。放眼望去，石峰林立，锷刺蓝天，有的像骆驼、大象，有的像苍龙、卧虎，有的像天桥、旗杆，有的像仙阁、楼观，随意联想，惟妙惟肖。尤其壮观的是，由于岩溶地貌套叠着冰川地貌，形成了角峰突兀，崖壁奇峭，冰川倒挂、万谷千壑的奇妙景象，真可谓造化之杰作，人间之奇观。

阿尔金山入山口　The pass of the Arjin Mountain

Karst Landscape

Located on the Age Mountain of the Arjin Mountain Nature Reserve, the Karst landscape abuts the Bukadaban Peak in the east and the Aqqikkol Lake in the west. With a length of 350 km and a width of 20 to 30 km, it covers a total area of some 10,000 square km at an elevation of 4,400 to 5,000 meters.

Karst is a distinctive landscape formed by the dissolution of limestone after being exposed to the rain and wind for thousands of years. Looking from afar, the sky-piercing rocks resemble various figures, such as a tame camel, giant elephant, flying dragon, crouching tiger, magnificent bridge and delicate pavilion. As far as you can imagine, you can find any thing you like in this wonderful land. Although karst is not rare in China, the one in the Arjin Mountain Nature Reserve enjoys a salient feature unique to it, because in this area, there is a unique combination of the karst landscape and the glacier landscape. Walking through this area, visitors marvel at the natural stone masterpieces and are bewitched by the intricate limestone columns and lofty glaciers.

干涸的罗布泊　The dried up Lop Nur

阿尔金山自然保护区的沙子泉与沙子河
The Sand Spring and the Sand River in the Arjin Mountain Nature Reserve

阿尔金山高原沙漠

阿尔金山高原沙漠位于若羌县境南部阿尔金山自然保护区内，其中尤以库木库里沙漠和积沙滩新月形沙丘最为著名，为世界海拔最高的沙漠。

库木库里沙漠位于保护区的东北部，横卧在祁曼塔格山南麓，海拔在3916～4706米之间，总面积约2556平方公里，呈不规则长方形。沙漠厚度平均为300米，最大厚度500多米。一座座高大的金字塔式沙丘和复合形新月形沙丘巍峨林立，一片片绿洲点缀其间，实为高原大漠之奇观。

Plateau Desert

Plateau deserts on the Arjin Mountain range are mainly distributed in the Arjin Mountain Nature Reserve in the southern part of Ruoqiang County. Of all the deserts, the Koshikoli Desert and the lunette sand dunes of the Jishatan Desert are the most famous ones, for they are both among the highest deserts in the world.

The Koshikoli Desert lies in the northeastern part of the nature reserve, at the south foot of the Qimantage Mountain. The lowest part of the desert is 3,916 meters above sea level while the highest part is 4,706 meters above sea level. The desert covers a total area of 2,556 square km, spreading out like an irregular rectangle. On average, in this desert, the sand is 300 meters deep, and at the deepest point measures more than 500 meters. Dotted with evergreen oases, the desert is mostly covered by undulating sand dunes in various shapes like gigantic pyramids and crescents. The area boasts a magnificent vista unique to plateau deserts.

积沙滩新月形沙丘，位于鲸鱼湖以东，巍巍雪山以北，总面积120平方公里，海拔高度为4800～5000米之间，比号称世界第一高的沙漠—南美洲阿卡玛沙漠（海拔3000米左右）还要高出2000米左右。该沙漠活动性大，持续不断地堆积上升，掩埋了近代河床及冰积物。沙丘底部的潜水极为丰富，依地形汇集成水泊，状如月牙，故命名月牙泉。泉水夏季碧蓝清澈，冬季如倒映之银月，足可与敦煌鸣沙山之月牙泉争奇斗艳。

The lunette sand dunes of the Jishatan Desert are located to the east of the amazing Jingyu Lake and to the north of the great mountains perennially covered by snow. With a total area of 120 square km, the sand dunes are 4,800 to 5,000 meters above sea level, some 2,000 meters higher than the Akarma Desert in South America, which is entitled as the world's highest desert with an elevation of approximately 3,000 meters. The landscape changes rapidly in this area. Sands are constantly deposited on the dunes so that the nearby riverbeds and moraines are all buried underneath. This area has a rich repository of ground water, which forms pools in the shape of crescents at the foot of the sand dunes. Also named Crescent Springs, the pools on the Arjin Mountain are on a par with the famous Crescent Spring in Dunhuang. In summer, crystal clear water ripples in the breeze, and in winter the freezing lake surface looks like mirrors under the silver moonlights at night.

阿尔金山老虎嘴
The Tiger Mouth of the Arjin Mountain

若羌红砖路
The red brick road in Ruoqiang

阿尔金山石棉矿全景
The panorama of the asbestos mine in the Arjin Mountain

阿尔金山魔鬼谷

阿尔金山魔鬼谷位于阿尔金山自然保护区南端，若羌县与青海省交界处的昆仑山区，它西起库木库西沙漠，东到布仑台，全长100公里，宽30公里，海拔3000～4000米。在这片3000平方公里的土地上，大小湖泊星罗棋布，那棱格勒河穿越其中，雨量充沛，气候湿润，草本繁茂，野花似锦，恰如一条绿色地毯。然而这片广袤的绿色土地，却被人们称为“魔鬼谷”，农夫不近，牧民远徙，成为荒无人烟的禁区，充满阴森恐怖的气氛。

Moguigu Valley (Devil's Valley)

The Moguigu Valley sits in the southern tip of the Arjin Mountain Nature Reserve, in the Kunlunshan Mountain range where Ruoqiang County borders Qinghai Province. The valley extends 100 km from the Koshiko Desert in the west to Bruntai in the east. It is 30 km wide, rising 3,000 to 4,000 meters high above sea level. The valley covers a total area of 3,000 square km. Lakes of various sizes are spread out all over it and the Nalenggele River runs through the area. With sufficient rainfall all year round, the Moguigu Valley has a humid climate and a dense distribution of plants. Full of thriving grass and flowers, it spreads out like a green belt under the high mountains. However, the beautiful land has a dreadful name. The Moguigu Valley, or the Devil's Valley, is notorious far and wide. In the past, no one dared to enter this place and the deserted valley was once shrouded in an impressively horrific atmosphere.

1949年中华人民共和国成立以来，组织科技人员对这里进行了考察，初步揭开了魔鬼谷的神秘面纱。其一是魔鬼谷南有高耸入云的昆仑山主脊，北有祁曼塔格山阻挡柴达木盆地炎热的空气，两山夹峙，使湿润的空气汇集魔鬼谷内，形成多雷雨天气。而魔鬼谷地质结构大多是强磁性玄武岩，还有大大小小30多个铁矿脉及石英体，再加上地下磁场的作用，经常产生“雷暴”现象，使突兀裸露的地面目标成为雷电袭击的对象；其二是魔鬼谷暗河多，泥沼多，每当春暖解冻，人畜往往会陷入被水草覆盖的泥沼或暗河，以此无人敢问其津，形成荒无人烟的神秘禁区。现在，科技工作者正在进一步探索研究，相信魔鬼谷的神秘之谜将会完全解开。

通往阿尔金山石棉矿的公路
The highway to the asbestos mine in the Arjin Mountain

Since the founding of the People's Republic of China in 1949, the Chinese government has sent groups of scientists into the valley to conduct research. After years of hard work, they managed to give an explanation of the mysterious phenomenon in the valley. One reason is that the Moguigu Valley is sandwiched between two high mountains. To its south, there is the main peak of the magnificent Kunlun Mountain. To its north, there is the Qimantage Mountain that blocks the hot air from the Qaidam Basin. Humid air accumulates in the valley and results in frequent thunder showers. Furthermore, the valley is mainly composed of strongly magnetic basalts, along with some 30 large or small deposits of iron ore and quartz. Under the impact of underground magnetic fields, the humid air and the magnetic rocks combine to create horrible thunderstorms, which will strike any object erected on the nearby ground. The other reason for the strange phenomenon in the Moguigu Valley is that there are a huge number of underground rivers and swamps. These rivers and swamps thaw in the spring but since they are mostly well covered by thick grass, humans and animals sometimes fall into them accidentally. In the past, no one dared to enter the valley to solve the mysterious disappearance of men and animals, and the valley gradually grew into a deserted land wrapped in a shroud of mystery. Today, thanks to the hard work of scientists, the true story of the Moguigu Valley is finally revealed.

晨曦中的慕士塔格峰　The dawn of the Muztag Ata

祁曼塔格山的怪石　Odd rocks in the Qimantage mountain

阿尔金山地震大断层

阿尔金山地震大断层断裂带长近1000公里，宽数百公里，属走滑型活断层带。这样的断层区域理应频发较大的地震，然而这里却很少发生，以此引起了中外专家对阿尔金山大断层的极大兴趣。

Great Earthquake Fault

The great earthquake fault on the Arjin Mountain extends approximately 1,000 km, with a width of hundreds of km. As an active strike-slip fault, it is very likely to cause powerful earthquakes. However, the Arjin Mountain range has remained peaceful and safe over the passage of time. Such an unusual phenomenon attracts great attention from geologists at home and abroad.

阿尔金山细石器遗址

阿尔金山细石器遗址分布在阿尔金山自然保护区内的库鲁克皮特勒克塔格山脚一带和喀尔墩、野牛泉等处。库鲁克皮特勒克塔格山脚遗址，地处东经90° 15’，北纬36° 44’；野牛泉遗址，东经 87° 54’ 30”，北纬36° 53’ 45”。在野牛泉以东约200公里处的同纬度地区是喀尔墩遗址。三处遗址的海拔均在4300米以上，干旱寒冷，空气稀薄，生态环境严酷，千里杳无人烟。但考古工作者在这些地方发现并采集了相当丰富的细石器标本，有石核、刮削器、小石叶、石镞、刃片等，这些标本现在大部分被珍藏于自治区博物馆和新疆考古研究所。石器用料以燧石和水晶石为主，经过打制并压修加工，具有明显的早期文化特点。

阿尔金山 The Arjin Mountain

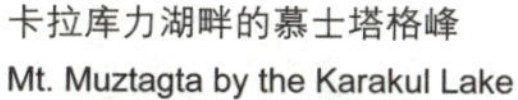

卡拉库力湖畔的慕士塔格峰
Mt. Muztagta by the Karakul Lake

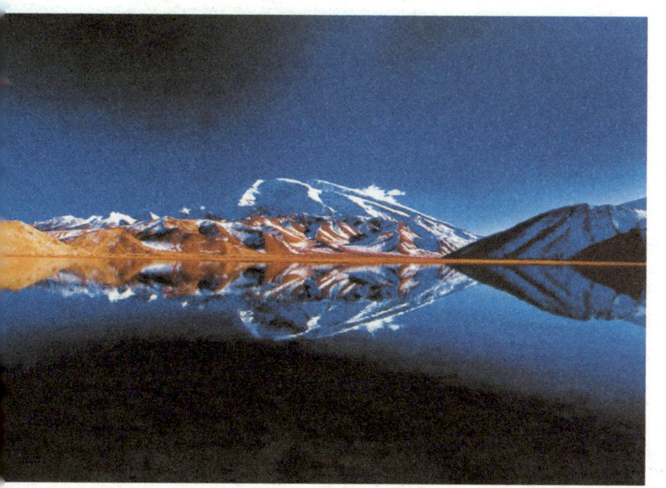

Relics of Mircolithic Culture

Relics of microlithic culture in the Arjin Nature Reserve are mainly distributed at the foot of the Kuluk Pitelek Tage Mountain, Kardun and the Yeniuquan Spring (Wild Ox Spring). Of them, the one under the Kuluk Pitelek Tage Mountain lies at 90°15’ east and 36°44’ north, the one near the Yeniuquan Spring (Wild Ox Spring) is found at 87°54’30” east and 36°53’45” north, and the one in Kardun is some 200 km to the east of the Yeniuquan Spring (Wild Ox Spring) at the same latitude. All of the three relics rise 4,300 meters above sea level. With harsh natural conditions featuring dry, chilly and thin air, the place has been deserted for a long time, until recently a group of bold archeologists arrived and unearthed a variety of microlithic relics, including stone cores, flakes, arrowheads and blades. Most of the historical relics are now housed in the Xinjiang Museum and the Xinjiang Institute of Archeology. Mainly made of flint and quartz, these artifacts show salient features of primitive culture obvious in the cutting and polishing.

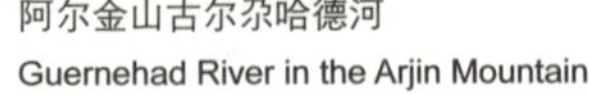

阿尔金山古尔尕哈德河

Guernehad River in the Arjin Mountain

阿尔金山盐湖

The salt lake in the Arjin Mountain

阿尔金山的河

阿尔金山保护区内主要有8条河流，组成了高原盆地中的“大动脉”，滋润着广阔的高山草场。8条主要河流的流域面积达两万平方公里。河流的水量补给主要有两种即冰川融水和出露泉水。保护区内河流形态各异，直泻湖盆。有的时而潜入地下，时而冒出地面，缓缓向盆地洼地汇集；有的水质纯洁；有的矿化度高达71.5克/升。苏鲁贝提勒克河为保护区最大的河流，源于新青峰北坡，注入阿牙克库木湖，全长280公里，流域面积达6250平方公里。保护区内湖泊星罗棋布，总面积1200平方公里，占保护区面积的2.7%，对调节区内气候起着至关重要的作用。

Rivers

The Arjin Mountain Nature Reserve has eight major rivers, which combine to form the “artery” of the plateau basin and nourish all the livings on this land. With a drainage area of 20,000 square km, the eight rivers pool waters from nearby melted ice and springs. Careening and twisting forward, they all pour down into the lakes at the bottom of the basin. Sometimes, a river may disappear from sight for a while and then suddenly gush out a distance away. Some of the rivers boast extremely pure water, while some have 71.5 grams of minerals in every liter of water. The Sulubeitilek River is the largest river in the Arjin Mountain Nature Reserve, with its headwater on the northern slope of the Xinqingfen. The river runs 280 km before it eventually pours into the Ayakkushi Lake. Areas drained by the Sulubeitilek River extend 6,250 square km. The nature reserve is dotted with lakes of all sizes and shapes. Covering 1,200 square km, they make up 2.7 percent of the total area of the nature reserve. These lakes play a significant role in adjusting the climate in the plateau basin.

卧龙湾
Crouching Dragon Bay

黑颈鹤
Black-necked crane

The Ayakkushi Lake is situated in the northern part of the nature reserve. It is recognized as the largest lake in this area, with an area of 536 square km. The Aqqikkol Lake lies in the western part of the nature reserve. In this 352-square-km lake, you can find 81.6 grams of mineral in every liter of water. In the middle of the Aqqikkol Lake, there are two islets that look like two vessels braving the winds and the waves. Flocks of birds inhabit the islets. The Jingyuhu Lake, or the Whale Lake, sits in the southern part of the nature reserve. The lake gets its name because it spreads out in the shape of a whale. The Kushi Lake and Kechik Kushi Lake, which mean "sand lake" and "little sand lake" in the Uygur language, are located on the Kushikuli Sand Mountain. Waters in these two lakes come from the water condensed on sand dunes and from the water seeping through cracks in the bedrock. The Kushi Lake and KechikKushi Lake enjoy a good water quality, with merely 0.3 grams of minerals in every liter of waters. The Yinchinpada Lake, also named the Yishiekpati Lake, is a freshwater lake and it is the only one in this area that has inlets and outlets. Covering an area of 11.8 square km, the lake is shaped like a gourd. Water in this lake is of good quality and the lake is a dark green color since it is home to a wide range of aquatic organisms like gammarid. In the Arjin Mountain Nature Reserve, the area near Yinchinpada Lake is the only place inhabited by herdsmen. The lake is also called the "paradise of birds".

阿牙克库木湖位于保护区北部，面积536平方公里，是保护区内面积最大的湖泊，阿其克库勒湖位于保护区西部，面积352平方公里，矿化度81.6克／升，湖中屹立着两个小岛，远远望去，犹如劈波斩浪前进的舰艇。岛上居住着大量的鸟群。鲸鱼湖位于保护区南部，以形似鲸鱼而得名。库木湖和克其克库木湖，维吾尔语称“沙子湖”和“小沙子湖”，位于库木库里沙山上；湖水为沙山凝聚水和基岩裂隙水补给，水质良好，矿化度为0.3克／升，唯一有进出口水的淡水湖伊阡巴达湖，又称“依协克帕提湖”，面积11.8平方公里，形如葫芦，水质较好，湖中生长着钩虾等多种水生生物，湖周围一片葱绿，这里是保护区内唯一有牧民居住的地方，也是“鸟类的天堂”。

阿尔金山的湖

积沙滩小湖群在沙丘链分隔的海拔4900米高的沙漠中，呈月牙形分布着145个小湖泊，保护区内还有多处冰河期残留的冰川终碛湖。受构造断裂裂隙控水作用和断层阻水影响，保护区南北侧地下水量差异很大，沿断裂走向南侧，有多处断裂泉。在石灰岩底层涌出的泉水，是很好的地下水资源。保护区东北部库木库里沙山北麓坡角的沙子泉，有3口高在3920米的泉眼，其东、南、西三面被沙山环绕，呈向北开口的漏斗。最大的泉眼直径在200米以上，其它两口为50米。泉水为下降泉特点，由坡角一线以数千股散流溢出，若人立泉水中，动则下陷。明布拉克，即“千泉”之意，因山中近千口泉眼散布在洼地边缘而得名。这里水草丰茂，是动物寻食的好场所。其火山活动区，尚有多处待探明的高山温泉。

阿尔金山 阿奇库克湖
The Aqikuke Lake in the Arjin Mountain

阿尔金山野牦牛
Wild yak in the Arjin Mountain

Lakes

On the Jishatan Desert at an elevation of 4,900 meters, there is a lake cluster composed of 145 lakes that spread out like a crescent. These lakes are separated from each other by strings of sand dunes. In the Arjin Mountain Nature Reserve, there are several remnants of moraine dammed lakes from the ice age. The quality of the ground water differs most greatly in the southern part and in northern part. This is mainly caused by the water seeping through tectonic cracks and the impact of a water resistant fault. Walking southward along the fault, you can find several springs gushing out through the cracks. Springs that well up from the bottom of the underground limestone are recognized as a precious water resource. The Shaziquan Spring (Sand Spring) lies at the northern foot of the Kushikuli Sand Mountain in the northeastern part of the nature reserve. The spring has three mouths, all of which rise 3,920 meters above sea level. Surrounded by sand hills in the east, south and west sides, the spring runs northward in the shape of funnel. The diameter of the largest spring mouth measures some 200 meters and that of the other two 50 meters. Waters from the three spring mouths flow gently at the foot of the hill but soon join with each other and grow into a large river. The Shaziquan Spring is a typical descending spring, with nearby water surface lower the spring mouth. Anyone who dares to step into the spring will sink with the slightest move. Ming Bulake means “a thousand springs” in the Uygur language. This area gets such a name because there are almost 1,000 springs scattered along the rim of the basin. With plentiful water and lush grass, this area offers food for numerous animals and there are several alpine hot springs in the volcano-active area.

鲸鱼湖奇景

在若羌县东南部的昆仑山腹地，平卧着一个神奇的大湖，它东西长37公里，南北宽7.6公里，面积260平方公里，湖面海拔高达4708米，湖深1－10米。湖水与雪山冰峰相互辉映，湖的形状恰似一条横卧着的肥大鲸鱼，头东尾西，故而得名“鲸鱼湖”。湖的东段七分之一处，形成了一道长达7.5公里的自然砂砾堤，将湖水自然的分隔成东、西两部分。砂砾堤宽约200米，高出湖面2－4米，中间有缺口，两侧之水可以互通。东半湖“鱼头处”因有玉浪河流人而带来各种鱼类和水草，每年夏季，都有无数的棕头鸥和赤麻鸭等飞禽在此觅食繁育。西半湖“鱼身处”因无淡水补给，天长日久，蒸发强烈，湖水含盐量几乎达到饱和状态，是一个没有生命的死湖。由于两湖水质差异明显，自然形成东湖“鸥歌鸭舞”、西湖“万马齐喑”的鲜明对比，因此，人们又把鲸鱼湖叫做“阴阳湖”。

阿尔金山祁曼塔格乡

The Qimantage Township in the Arjin Mountain

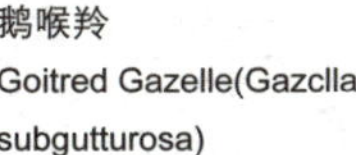

鹅喉羚
Goitred Gazelle(Gazclla subgutturosa)

Jingyuhu Lake (Whale Lake)

In the hinterland of the Kunlunshan Mountain range to the southeast of Ruoqiang County, a magic lake extends 37 km from east to west and 7.6 km from south to north. Covering an area of 260 square km, the lake is 4,708 meters above sea level. While the shallowest part measures only one meter, the deepest part of measures 10 meters. The rippling lake and the nearby snow-covered peaks combine to form a beautiful scene. The lake is called Jingyuhu Lake, or the Whale Lake, for it is in the shape of a whale with its head toward the east and its tail toward the west. Near the eastern tip of the lake, a long heap of pebbles zigzags 75 km from the south bank to the north bank. These pebbles form a natural dyke and cut the lake into two parts. With a width of 200 meters, the wonderful dyke is two to four meters high above the surface of the lake. There is a gap in the dyke, allowing water to run between the eastern part and the western part of the lake. The eastern part of the lake is the "head of the whale". Here the Yulang River joins the Jingyuhu Lake and turns the eastern part into a freshwater lake. Every summer, flocks of birds like brown-headed gull and ruddy shelduck will settle down here to lay eggs. In comparison, the western part, or the "body of the whale", is a dead lake without any sign of life. Since there is no supply of fresh water, water in this part of the lake is saturated with salt. The two parts of the Jinyuhu Lake differ drastically with one full of the sights and sounds of life and the other deadly silent. Stunned by such a special scene, people also give the lake another name: the Lake of Yin and Yang.

阿尔金山上的岩羊　Blue sheep on the Arjin Mountain

野骆驼

野骆驼，别名野生双峰驼，属于骆驼科。大型偶蹄类。躯体高大，与家养双峰驼十分相似。其头小，耳短，上唇中央有裂，鼻孔内有瓣膜可防风沙。背具双驼峰，尾较短。四肢细长，脚掌下有宽厚的肉垫。全身被以细密而柔软的绒毛，毛色多为淡棕黄色，吻部毛色稍灰，肘关节处的毛尖呈棕黑色，尾毛棕黄色。

几百万年以前，骆驼的祖先住在北美亚利桑那沙漠中。它们只有1米左右高。在100多年以前，全世界皆认为野骆驼基本灭绝了。1883年，俄国探险家普热瓦尔斯基在罗布泊发现了野骆驼，并命名为“野生双峰驼西部亚种”。当时的罗布泊荒漠中常常出没着成群结队的野骆驼。

Wild Camel

Wild camel, or wild Bactrian camel, is a member of the family Camelidae in the order Artiodactyla. As strong and heavily built as the domesticated ones, the wild camel has a small head with a pair of short ears. The upper lip of the wild camel has a crack. The sealable nostrils form an effective barrier against sand. A wild camel has two humps, a short tail, four slim legs and a sturdy pad under each of its hoofs. Most wild camels are covered with light brown hairs that are soft but thick. In most cases, hairs near the mouth of a wild camel are a little grey, that near the elbows dark brown, and that on the tail pale brown.

Millions of years ago, the ancestors of camels lived in the Arizona Desert in North America. At that time, they were only one meter tall. Wild camels used to be on the list of extinct animals some 100 years ago until in 1883, a Russian adventurer discovered a wild camel in Lop Nur, where herds of wild camels had been living and multiplying over the centuries.

野骆驼
Bactriau camel

藏野驴　Tibetan wild donkey (Equus kiang)

历史上，整个中亚到西亚东部的低海拔丘陵及平原地区，西起里海东至陕西黄河，南到青藏高原北部，北抵贝加尔湖，皆有野骆驼分布。今天残存的只有4个分布区：罗布泊北部嘎顺戈壁分布有100峰左右；新疆阿尔金山北麓和甘肃阿克塞安南坝交界处、塔克拉玛干沙漠东部分布有300峰左右；甘肃阿克塞境内和敦煌湾腰墩有300峰左右；新疆哈密地区西北到北塔山与蒙古国交界地带，有100峰左右的野骆驼。100年前，野骆驼还有1万多峰。如今，国家一级保护野生动物野骆驼已十分稀少，亟待加强保护。

祁曼塔格山的怪石（组图） Odd rocks in the Qimantage Mountain

Historically, wild camels were widely distributed in the low-lying hilly area and plains of Central Asia and the eastern part of West Asia, a wide area extending to the Caspian Sea in the west and the Yellow River in China's Shaanxi Province in the east, and to the northern part of China's Qinghai-Tibet Plateau in the south to Russia's Beikal Lake in the north. Today, we can only find wild camels in four regions: the Garshun Gobi in the northern part of Lop Nur, the eastern part of the Taklimakan Desert and the juncture area of the Arjin Mountain of Xinjiang Uygur Autonomous Region and the Annanba Dam of Aksei of Gansu Province, Aksei and Dunhuang in Gansu Province, as well as the northern part of Xinjiang Hami area and the border area between China's Beita Mountain and the State of Mongolia. Wild camels once numbered 10,000 some 100 years ago. Today, however, in the above mentioned four regions, the number is reduced to 100, 300, 300 and 100 respectively. Wild camels are now under the first class State protection and more measures will to be adopted to protect this rare animal.

祁曼塔格山的怪石
Odd rocks in the Qimantage mountain

鹅喉羚 Goitred Gazelle (Gazclla subgutturosa)

★野骆驼的主要特点

野骆驼躯体高大，胆小机警，跑得快，每小时25千米左右。野骆驼的基因链比家骆驼多2－3个。最奇特之处还在于它能靠喝盐水生存。野骆驼驼峰主要是脂肪和结缔组织组成。隆起时蓄积量高达50千克，在饥饿和营养缺乏时则逐渐转化为身体所需的热能。野骆驼的嗅觉十分灵敏，在沙暴来临之前，野骆驼会尽快逃离。沙暴中沙子与石头乱飞，聪明的野骆驼如果来不及躲开就会躺在地上。野骆驼会掉眼泪，它那长长的睫毛下经常会流下一串串的泪水。其实它并不是真正的流泪，而是为洗刷沙尘保护眼睛。野骆驼的食物多种多样，沙漠中生长的盐生草、梭梭草、狼草、芦苇。沙拐枣、骆驼刺、红柳之类的沙生植物都是野骆驼充饥的食粮。野骆驼的另一个有趣之处就是，几百年来它能够沿着同一条道路迁徙。在沙漠中迤逦行走时，成年骆驼走在前面和后面，小骆驼则排在中间，并常常沿着固定的几条路线觅食和饮水，称为“骆驼小道”。

★ Major Features

Wild camels are usually heavily built but have a timid and cautious nature. Adept at running, they can reach a speed of 25 km per hour. A wild camel has two or three genetic chains more than domesticated camels. The most marvelous feature of wild camels is that they can subsist on merely salt water. The hump of a wild camel is mainly composed of fat and connective tissues. When the hump rises to its highest point, there will be 50 kilograms of fat, which will transform into energy when there is a deficiency of food. Wild camels have a keen sense of smell, which will lead them to escape from sandstorms beforehand. Wild camels are also intelligent. When they are trapped by sandstorms accidentally, they will lie down on the ground to reduce harm from flying sand and pebbles. Sometimes, tears will drop from the eyes of the wild camels. This is not because the camels are crying, but because they use tears to wash down the sand near their eyes. Wild camels can live on many foods, such as the halogeton, reeds, calligonum, Alhagi maurorum and red willow, all of which are common in deserts. Another interesting feature of the wild camel is that generations of wild camels in one herd can migrate along the same path for hundreds of years. When they trudge through the vast desert, they will form a line with the adult camels at the two ends and the young camels in the middle. They always walk along fixed paths and stop to take food and drink water at particular places. The paths they take are generally called the "camel path".

藏野驴
Tibetan wild donkey
(Equus kiang)

每到冬天，野骆驼成群结队地迁离阿尔金山，奔向罗布泊越冬。野骆驼有极强的交配和生殖能力。发情交配季节在每年冬末的1－3月，怀孕期为13个月，翌年2－4月生产，每胎产1仔，母骆驼对小骆驼呵护备至。幼骆驼出生2小时后便能站立。1年多以后小骆驼就完全可以独立生活了。幼骆驼一旦到了两岁龄左右，就会被逐出种群，去别的种群争夺“领导权”。4～5岁时性成熟。寿命为30～40年。雌性每2年繁殖一次。

阿尔金山国际狩猎场

狩猎场位于距且末县城150公里的阿尔金山北麓的塔特勒克苏与江尕勒萨依之间地区，平均海拔在3000米左右，面积为100平方公里，山体陡峭，剥蚀严重。山地植被有昆仑蒿、昆仑针茅、芨芨草等。河谷地带长有胡杨、芦苇、拂子茅、唐克特百刺。1993年4月26日国家林业部正式批准成立阿尔金山狩猎区且末猎场。狩猎场对国内外游客开放，狩猎者办理应有手续就可进入。西班牙游客瓦兰丁先生是狩猎场的第一位狩猎者。

野牦牛　Wild yak

Every winter, herds of wild camels will leave the Arjin Mountain to live in Lop Nur. Wild camels have a strong reproductive capacity. They tend to display interest in mating from January to March. Pregnancy usually lasts 13 months and a female camel will give birth to one baby in the following year between February and April. Female camels often devote special care to the new born camels. Wild camels can stand up two hours after birth and can live independently one year later. At the age of two, young camels will be driven out of their family herd to compete for the leadership in other herds. Wild camels are sexually mature at about four or five years old. Expected lifespan is 30 to 40 years and the breeding cycle of a female camel is two years.

Arjin Mountain International Hunting Ground

Some 150 km from Qiemo County, the hunting ground is situated between Tartlerksu and Jianggalesayi, at the north foot of the Arjin Mountain range. With an average elevation of 3,000 meters, the hunting ground covers an area of 100 square km. Mountains here are high and steep but cliffs have suffered severe erosion. The ground is covered by typical alpine plants. In the river valleys, you can find populus euphratica, reeds and calamagrostis epigejos. The Qiemo Hunting Ground of the Arjin Mountain International Hunting Region was set up on April 26, 1993 upon the approval of the Ministry of Forestry. As an international hunting ground, it is open to both Chinese and foreign tourists. Anyone can enter the ground after going through required procedures. A gentleman from Spain was the first hunter of the hunting ground.

附录

若羌距阿尔金山有280公里左右。从若羌出来有5公里的柏油路，此后全是颠簸的石子路。如果沿315国道通过石棉矿（新芒崖镇）前往阿尔金山，大约213公里左右到石棉矿，之后开始进入便道，石棉矿距离阿尔金山还有约200公里。

翻过一座固定沙丘，继续沿沙漠便道走就可以陆续见到各种野生动物了，并且这里已经靠近阿牙克库木湖——去阿尔金山的必经之路，沙漠便道紧沿着湖岸。这是条便道，不太好认。湖边的库木库里乡是这一地区惟一有人居住的地方，只有十来户维吾尔族牧民，都不通汉语，乡上有一所林业管理站，可以在乡上找老乡作向导再上山。

藏野驴　Tibetan wild donkey (Eguus Kiang)

岩羊　Blue sheep

Appendix

Ruoqiang County is some 280 km from the Arjin Mountain. There is a five-km long asphalt road outside the county and the ground turns bumpy afterwards. The No. 315 National Highway will lead you to the Asbesto Mine (Xinmangya Town) 213 km away. Here, you will enter a makeshift road and the Arjin Mountain is some 200 km away.

After getting over a fixed sand dune at the half way point of the makeshift road, you will see all kinds of wild animals running on the vast desert. The road is built along the bank of the Ayakkushi Lake and it is the only path to the Arjin Mountain. However, you may find some difficulties in recognizing the road since it is only built for temporary use and there are no commonly seen road facilities. The Kushikuli Township is located near the lake. This is the only human-inhabited area in this region. All of the villagers, some ten households of Uygur herdsmen, are unable to speak mandarin. There is a forestry station in the county. You can employ a herdsmen here as your mountain guide.

区内仅有一处林业管理站有招待所，价格昂贵，也可住老乡家，但价格面议。如果旅行者在此扎营，应注意安全。

1．阿尔金山自然保护区地形复杂、路况不好、景点众多，危险性较大，另外还要注意可能的高原反应。

2．前往阿尔金山考察或旅行都必须经过政府部门的许可，并在周密的计划和适当的组织下进行，切勿贸然进入。

如果需要紧急援助，可以就近向这两个单位联系：若羌县阿尔金出自然保护区管理站（0996－7102811），若羌县祁曼塔格乡派出所。工作人员大多有行走阿尔金山的丰富经验。

在去阿尔金山的路上，只有石棉矿和若羌有加油站，需要准备充足的汽油、轮胎及其他配件。此外，还应准备充分的食物与水、全套野外宿营装备等。

这里属于典型的荒漠高原气候，紫外线强烈，时有暴雨，昼夜温差很大，最佳参观季节为6～9月。

雪鸡　Snow cock

In this area, there is only one hostel run by the forestry station with an expensive accommodation fee. You can also live in the houses of local villagers, but there is no fixed price and how much you pay depends on your ability to negotiate. If you prefer to make camp here, please be careful.

1. The Arjin Mountain Nature Reserve boasts a variety of beautiful scenery, but this area is also a dangerous place with complicated landscapes and rough road conditions. Some tourists may develop altitude sickness.

2. Any scientific investigation or travel should be applied to proper authorities for approval. There should be a well-conceived plan and adequate preparations. It is unwise to take any rash action in this region.

For emergency aid, please contact the following two units: the Ruoqiang Administration Center of the Arjin Mountain Nature Reserve (tele: 0996-7102811), and the Police Station of Chimantage Township of Ruoqiang County. Staff members of these two units are all experienced mountain climbers.

Please make sure you have enough gasoline, spare tire and other necessary components on your car before you start the journey. On your way to the Arjin Mountain, you can find gas stations only in the Asbesto Mine and Ruoqiang County. Sufficient food and water, and a whole set of camp facilities are also necessary.

The Arjin Mountain belongs to the typical desert plateau climate. With strong sunshine and frequent heavy rain, the area sees great difference in temperature between day and night. The best time to tour around the area is between June and September.

雕　Eagle

克孜尔千佛洞

KEZIER THOUSAND-BUDDHA GROTTOES

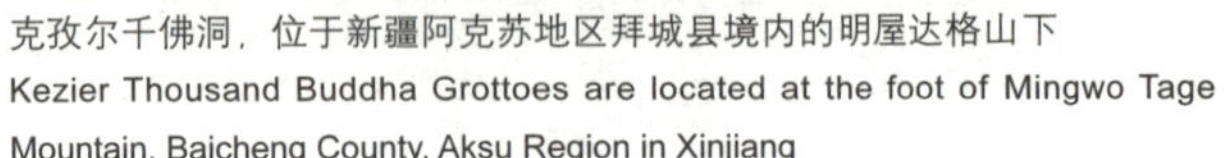
克孜尔千佛洞，位于新疆阿克苏地区拜城县境内的明屋达格山下
Kezier Thousand Buddha Grottoes are located at the foot of Mingwo Tage Mountain, Baicheng County, Aksu Region in Xinjiang

克孜尔千佛洞局部
One area of Kezier Thousand Buddha Grottoes

克孜尔千佛洞，是中国国家重点文物保护单位，著名的佛教圣地，丝绸之路上一颗璀璨的明珠。位于新疆阿克苏地区拜城县境内的明屋达格山下，木扎提河（发源于天山最高峰托木尔峰）从其南面蜿蜒东流，给这片小小的绿洲带来了无限生机与活力。石窟与河南岸的雀尔达格山遥遥相望，距库车67千米。

古人选择在这里建造石窟自有其道理。佛经上规定，僧徒修道的场所，既不能靠近众人喧闹的城镇，影响他们的宗教生活，也不能离城镇太远，断了人间烟火，衣食没有保障。这里地理位置适中，又有优越的自然条件，是建造石窟的最理想的场所。

Kezier (Bezeklik) Thousand-Buddha Grottoes, a key state protection unit of cultural relics in China, is a famous Buddhist Holy Land and a brilliant pearl on the Silk Road. It is located at the foot of the Mingwo Tage Mountain within the territory of Baicheng County in Aksu Region in Xinjiang, and the Mozhati River (which originates from the highest peak, Tomor Peak, of the Tianshan Mountain) zigzags from south to east zigzag bringing limitless vigor and energy to this small oasis. The Grotto faces the Ch'er Tage Mountain far away on the southern bank of the river and is 67 km from Kuche.

Ancient people of course had reasons for building grottoes here. According to instructions in sutras, the sites for monks to cultivate themselves could not be close to busy towns which might affect their religious life, or too far away from towns, which might cut off the provision of food and clothes from the outside world. The geographic position there is moderate and, with excellent natural conditions, it is an ideal place to build grottoes.

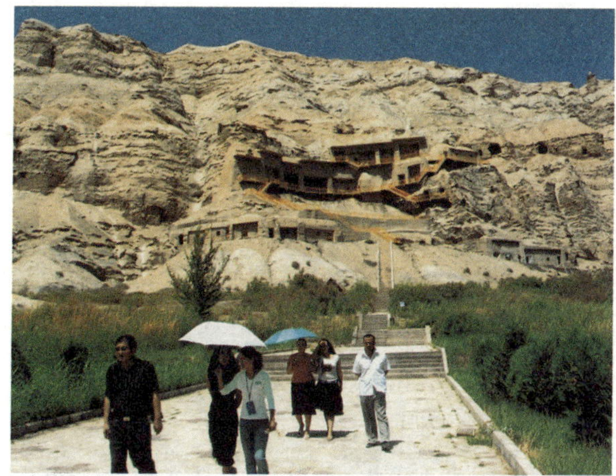

每年前来游览的游客络绎不绝
Many people pay a visit to the Grottoes every year.

According to historical records and analysis of the spreading of Buddhism in ancient Kucha, the building of Kezier Thousand-Buddha Grottoes started in the 3rd or 4th century or even earlier, reached prosperity in the 6th to 7th century and was gradually abandoned at the end of the 8th century when Tubo occupied Kucha and the large-scale construction of the grotto was stopped. The time of construction lasted for five or six hundred years.

Kezier Thousand-Buddha Grottoes is the grotto which is farthest west among the Four Great Grottoes in China (i.e. Dunhuang Grotto, Longmen Grotto, Yungang Grotto and Kezier Thousand-Buddha Grottoes) and the large-scale thousand-Buddha grottoes with the longest history in China. As the largest Buddhist cultural relic in Xinjing, Kezier Thousand-Buddha Grottoes has 236 grottoes cleaned up and numbered, including "Zhiti Grotto" for offering sacrifice to Buddha Figures and doing divine service, "Picolo Grotto", an exquisite room for monks to cultivate themselves quietly or give lectures, "small houses" as living quarters for monks, "Arhat Grotto" for burying bone ash, and warehouses for storing food. It is a rare scene among grottoes groups to have such a complete architectural structure.

根据史书记载以及佛教在古龟兹流传的情况来分析，克孜尔千佛洞大约始建于公元3－4世纪，或者更早一些；其兴盛期在公元6－7世纪；8世纪末吐蕃占据龟兹后可能已逐步废弃，至少可以说此时已停止大规模的兴建，其相继营造的时间长达五六百年之久。

克孜尔千佛洞是我国四大石窟（敦煌石窟、龙门石窟、云冈石窟、克孜尔千佛洞）中地理位置最西的一个，也是中国现存最早的大型千佛洞。克孜尔千佛洞作为新疆最大的一处佛教文化遗址，现己清理编号的洞窟有236个，包括供养佛像作礼拜用的“支提窟”，僧尼静修或讲学用的精舍“毗呵罗窟”，僧尼起居用的“寮房”，埋葬骨灰用的“罗汉窟”，以及储存食物用的仓库等。其保存如此完整的建筑格局，在其它石窟群中是少见的。

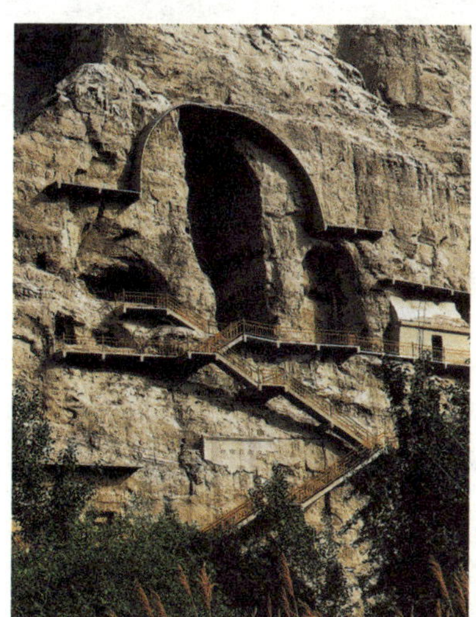

克孜尔千佛洞西区
The west side of the Kezier Thousand Buddha Grottoes

克孜尔千佛洞全景
Panoramic view of the Kezier Thousand Buddha Grottoes

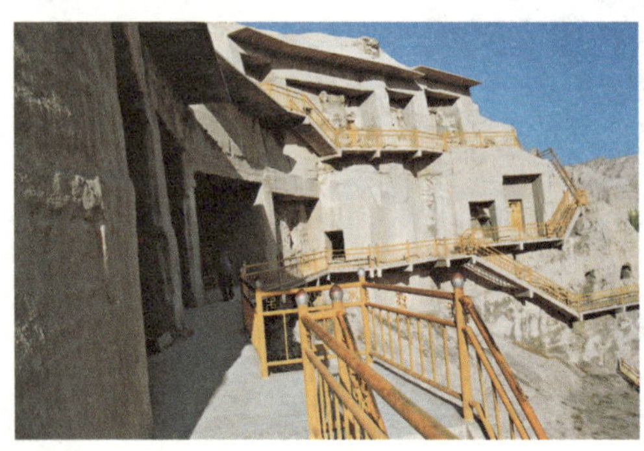

克孜尔千佛洞局部
One area of the Kezier Thousand Buddha Grottoes

克孜尔千佛洞陶祖
Clay phallus unearthed at the Kezier Thousand Buddha Grottoes

克孜尔千佛洞保存壁画面积近一万平方米，是世界上仅次于敦煌石窟的壁画宝库。壁画内容除佛像、菩萨、天龙八部、罗汉、佛传故事、佛本生故事、经变、飞天、伎乐天外，还有大量的以山水花鸟、飞禽走兽、供养人、生产和生活场面为题材的民间民俗画。古代龟兹画师们技艺高超，“湿画法”就是他们的杰出创造。在泥壁上直接作画，而不是画在涂白的墙壁上，既使用透明颜料，也使用有覆盖力的矿物颜料。着色时，不仅使用平涂和烘染，而且还借助水分在底壁上的晕散。这就是古代龟兹画师们创造的“湿画法”，也称凹凸画法。69号洞窟内的“龟兹王礼佛图”，就是“湿画法” 的代表作。古代画师们通过这些生动的画面，向我们展示了大约从公元3世纪到13世纪，古代新疆地区的历史风情与生活图景。这些珍贵的形象资料，对我们研究古代新疆的政治、文化、宗教、经济、军事、民族与民俗，以及古丝绸之路上中西经济、文化交流，具有极高的价值。

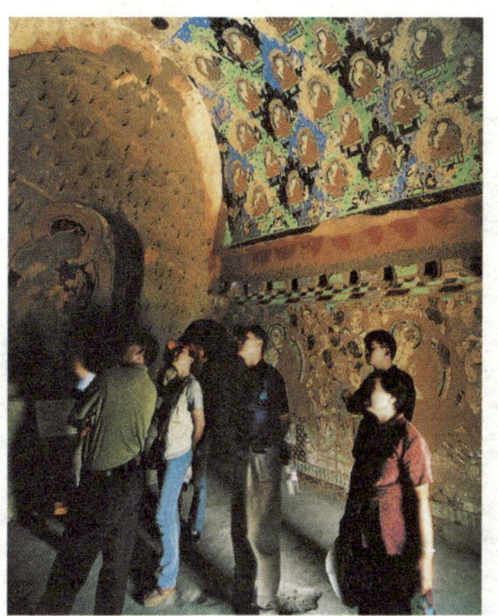

欣赏克孜尔千佛洞壁画
Visitors are appreciating the frescoes in the Grottoes

克孜尔千佛洞外景
The exterior of the Kezier Thousand Buddha Grottoes

Kezier Thousand-Buddha Grottoes contains nearly 10,000 square meters of mural paintings and it is the second largest treasury of mural paintings, only next to Dunhuang Grottoes, in the world. As to the contents of the mural paintings, there are many folk-custom paintings with the subjects of mountains, rivers, flowers, birds, animals, suppliers and scenes of daily life and work in addition to Buddha Figures, Bodhisattva, Demi-Gods and Semi-Devils, arhats, Buddhist stories, Buddhist jataka stories, illustrations of sutras, flying goddess, and Musical Fairies. The ancient Kucha painting masters had excellent skills and frescoes were their most outstanding creations. They painted directly on fresh mud walls instead of walls painted white. They not only used transparent pigment but also used mineral pigment that to add color. When coloring, they not only used flat painting and added shading around objects, but also made use of the demitint of water on the bottom of the wall. It is the fresco created by the ancient Kucha painting masters and it is also called concave and protruding painting. The “Picture of King of Kucha Worshipping Buddha” in No. 69 Grotto is the representative fresco. Through these vivid pictures, ancient painting masters showed us the historical customs and practices and living scenes in ancient Xinjiang region from the 3rd to 13th century. These precious images have supreme value in researching the politics, culture, religion, economy, military affairs, nationalities and folk customs in ancient Xinjiang and the economic and cultural exchanges between China and the West on the ancient Silk Road.

克孜尔千佛洞局部
One area of the Kezier Thousand Buddha Grottoes

克孜尔千佛洞第8窟壁画 飞天
Frescoes in the No.8th cave: Flying Apsaras

反映佛教经典的佛本生故事画，是克孜尔千佛洞的精华。克孜尔千佛洞的佛本生故事画不仅艺术水平高，独树一帜，而且数量也最多，大约有60至70多种，是敦煌、龙门、云冈三处石窟总和（30多种）的两倍多。在被誉为“故事画之冠”的第17号洞内，在供养佛像的“支提窟”内，四壁、窟顶、龛楣甬道，到处都是色彩艳丽的壁画，其中窟顶画有“萨博白毡缚臂，苏油灌之，点燃引路”的本生故事。尽管具有浓厚的宗教色彩，但仍可看出在古丝绸之路上，佛教僧侣与骆驼商队的密切关系。商旅需要僧侣为他们祈求平安，僧侣不仅需要商队的施舍，还往往与大型骆驼商队结伴同行，或去传经，或去求法。

The Buddhist jataka stories paintings reflecting Buddhist sutras are the elite of KezierThousand-Buddha Grottoes. The Buddhist jataka stories paintings in Kezier Thousand-Buddha Grottoes are not only of a high and unique artistic level but also the most numerous. There are about 60 to 70 varieties, more than double the sum (over 30 varieties) of those in Dunhuang, Longmen and Yungang Grottooes. In the No.17 grotto praised as the “champion of story paintings”, in the “Zhiti Grotto” where sacrifices are offered to Buddha Figures, mural paintings with bright colors are all over the surrounding walls, roof, shrines and walkways. On the grotto roof there is painted the jataka story that “Sabo used white felt to wrap around his arms and filled it with ghee for lighting to lead the way.” Notwithstanding the strong religious color, the paintings reflect the close relations between Buddhist monks and the camel trade caravans on the ancient Silk Road. Traveling businessmen needed the monks to pray for their safety, and the monks not only needed the alms from trade caravans but also wanted to travel with the large camel trade caravans to spread sutras or seek doctrines.

克孜尔千佛洞的壁画，不仅有众多的佛教题材的画面，也有反映农耕、畜牧、狩猎、车船、建筑的世俗题材壁画。175号洞窟内的“耕作图”，38号洞窟墙壁上的“龟兹乐舞图”就是表现世俗生活的佳作。早在公元1世纪，大约东汉明帝时期，佛教就经由丝绸之路传到了新疆地区，到公元13至14世纪伊斯兰教取代佛教止，佛教在新疆兴盛了一千余年。公元4世纪，佛教在龟兹王国既已兴盛，当时修建有大量装饰讲究、规模宏大的寺院及千佛洞。到公元7世纪，龟兹的佛教达到极盛。《大唐西域记》记载：“龟兹有佛寺一百余所，僧尼五千多人，每年秋分都要举行迎佛像大会十余日……。”克孜尔千佛洞内的大量壁画，就生动形象地展示了当时龟兹王世代信佛的实况。

Among the mural paintings in Kezier Thousand-Buddha Grottoes, there are numerous paintings reflecting Buddhist subjects, as well as those reflecting secular subjects such as farming, animal husbandry, hunting, vehicles and constructions. The “Farming Painting” in No. 175 Grotto and the “Kucha Singing and Dancing Painting” in No. 38 Grotto are excellent works reflecting secular life. As early as the 1st century during the time of Emperor Mingdi of the Eastern Han Dynasty, Buddhism was introduced to the region of Xinjiang via the Silk Road. Until the 13th to 14th century when Islam took the place of Buddhism, Buddhism had prospered in Xinjiang for more than a thousand years. In the 4th century Buddhism had become prevalent in the Kucha kingdom when a large number of temples and thousand-Buddha grottoes with excellent decorations and grand scale were built. In the 7th century Buddhism in Kucha reached its peak. According to the Records of the *Western Region of the Grand Tang Dynasty*, “There are more than 100 temples and more than 5,000 monks and nuns in Kucha. On the autumnal equinox every year a grand ceremony would be held for more than ten days to welcome Buddhist Figures...” Many mural paintings in Kezier Thousand-Buddha Grottoes vividly presented the actual scenes of believing in Buddhism for generations of kings of Kucha.

克孜尔千佛洞 烽燧
Beacon tower of the Kezier Thousand Buddha Grottoes

克孜尔菩提山庄
Kezier Bodhi Villa

克孜尔千佛洞第8窟壁画 供养人
Frescoes in the No.8th cave: The donors

The mural paintings in Kezier Thousand-Buddha Grottoes not only had the influence of the Han culture and the absorption of foreign cultural arts, but also contained the wisdom of Kucha painting masters. They combined the intelligence and wisdom of many nationalities. The building of Kezier Thousand-Buddha Grottoes started at the beginning of Chinese grotto art and is located at the thoroughfare on the Silk Road, so it witnessed the spreading of Buddhism and relevant arts to the surrounding areas.

Since the founding of the People's Republic of China in 1949, the people's government has attached importance to the protection and research work on the Kezier Thousand-Buddha Grottoes. In 1961 Kezier Thousand-Buddha Grottoes was listed as one of the first key cultural relic protection units in China and received proper protection. The modern day Kezier Thousand-Buddha Grottoes has developed into a research center of Buddhist art in Xinjiang and become a tourism scenic spot famous at home and abroad.

克孜尔千佛洞的壁画，既有汉文化的影响，也有对外来文化艺术的吸收，更有龟兹画师们的智慧。它凝聚了各族人民的聪明才智。克孜尔千佛洞开凿于中国石窟艺术首创时期，又地处丝绸之路的要冲，因此，它也是佛教及其有关艺术经这里传往内地的一个见证。

1949年中华人民共和国成立以来，人民政府十分重视对克孜尔千佛洞的保护和研究工作。1961年，克孜尔千佛洞被列为全国第一批重点文物保护单位之一，得到妥善的保护。现今的克孜尔千佛洞已建设成为新疆佛教艺术的研究中心，成为国内外著名的旅游胜地。

克孜尔千佛洞第14窟壁画 大光明王始发道心
Frescoes in the No. 14th cave: Mahaprabhasa adopted the policy of benevolence

近年，经过抢救和维护，克孜尔千佛洞的洞窟得到加固，新修的混凝土栈道和台阶取代了过去的木梯，这不仅极大地方便了参观者，同时也为他们的安全提供了保障。

静卧在明屋达格山脚下的克孜尔千佛洞，依然是那么安闲，静谧，它本身就是一部跌宕起伏的历史，见证着世事沧桑，向人们讲述着佛教的流传故事，古代龟兹国崇佛的故事，以及发生在丝绸之路上的故事，娓娓动听，栩栩如生，引人入胜。

In recent years after reclamation and maintenance, Kezier Thousand-Buddha Grottoes was upgraded with newly-built concrete plank roads and steps in place of the old wooden stairs, which not only offers more convenience to visitors but also provides them safety.

Lying quietly at the foot of the Mingwo Tage Mountain, Kezier Thousand-Buddha Grottoes is still leisurely and peaceful. It has a history full of ups and downs, witnessing the affairs and great changes of the world, and tells people the story of the spreading of Buddhism, the stories about worshipping Buddhism in ancient Kucha Kingdom and the stories of the Silk Road. They are charming, vivid and enchanting.

龟兹古渡　Ancient ferry crossing of Kucha

龟兹故城遗迹　The relics of ancient Kucha city

克孜尔千佛洞第17窟壁画 端正王智断儿案
Frescoes in the No. 17th cave: King Duanzheng wisely solved the dispute of two women over a son.

克孜尔第17窟壁画 卢舍那佛
Frescoes in the No. 17th cave: Rocana Buddha

克孜尔千佛洞第17窟 菱格本生故事壁画
Frescoes in the No. 17th cave: Jataka drawn in diamond panel

克孜尔千佛洞第17窟壁画 熊救樵人背恩
Frescoes in the No. 17th cave: The retribution of an ungrateful woodchopper who was ever saved by a bear.

佛本生故事

“本生”，巴利文Jataka的意译，音译为“陀伽”。意思是释迦牟尼如来佛前生的故事。古代印度相信轮回转生。一个动物，既然降生，必有所为，或善或恶，不出两途。有因必有果，这就决定了它们转生的好坏。如此轮回，永无止息。释迦牟尼在成佛以前，只是一个菩萨，他还跳不出轮回，必须经过无数次的转生，才能成佛。因此，就产生了所谓佛本生故事。

虽然佛本生讲述的是佛陀前生的故事，但实际上绝大部分是流传于古印度民间的寓言故事，佛教徒只是加以采集，并按照固定的格式，给每个故事加上头尾，指出其中的一个人、一个神仙或一只动物是佛陀的前身而已。每篇佛本生故事都由五个部分组成：(1) 今生故事——说明佛陀讲述前生故事的地点和缘由；(2) 前生故事——讲述佛陀的前生故事；(3) 偈颂诗——既有总结性质的，也有描述性质的，一般出现在前生故事中，有时也出现在今生故事中；(4) 注释——解释偈颂诗中的词义；(5) 对应——将前生故事中的角色与今生故事中的人物对应起来。

Buddhist Jataka Stories

Jataka is a Pali word meaning "stories of Buddha's previous incarnation". In ancient India people believed in samsara. After birth, any animal would do something good or evil, one or the other. Cause results in effect consequently, which decides whether their incarnation is to be good or bad. Such incarnation is endless. Before becoming a Buddha, Sakyamuni was just a Bodhisattva. He could not break away from incarnation and could only become a Buddha after countless times of incarnation, hence the stories about Buddhist jataka.

Jataka tells the stories about the pre-life of Buddha, but actually most of the stories are fables spread among the people of ancient India. Buddhist believers just gathered these stories, added beginnings and endings in fixed forms to each story and pointed out a person, an immortal or an animal that was the pre-life of Buddha. Each jataka story is composed of five parts: 1, the story of this life, explaining the place and cause to explain the pre-life of Buddha; 2, the story of pre-life, telling the pre-life story of Buddha; 3, chanted poem, it is conclusive or descriptive and often appears in the pre-life story or sometimes in the story of this life; 4, annotation, interpreting the meaning of words in the chanted poem; and 5, correspondence, corresponding a character in the pre-life story with the figure in the story of this life.

克孜尔千佛洞第17窟壁画 象王舍身救猎师
Frescoes in the No.17th cave: King Elephant scarified himself to save a master of hunting.

克孜尔千佛洞第17窟壁画 修楼婆王闻法舍妻儿
Frescoes in the No.17th cave: King Suloupo contributed his wife and son after hearing the preaching of Buddha

石窟中的佛本生故事画不是采用卷轴连环画的构图形式，它只是撷取佛本生故事中最精彩的一个场面在绘画中予以表现。因此它好比是一个特写镜头，摄取了本生故事中的精髓，抓住了本生故事中最本质的东西，用色彩集其艺术之美于一点而加以再现。总的来说，石窟的佛本生故事画，用笔粗疏，色调清淡，形象洗练，风格简朴。

The jataka story paintings in grottoes are not in the form of scroll paintings but the expression of the most magnificent scenes from the Buddhist jataka stories. So a painting seems like a close-up, shooting the soul of a jataka story, grasping the essence of a jataka story, and reproducing it with colors and artistic beauty. In a word, the Buddhist jataka story paintings in grottoes are in careless lines with light colors, compact images and simple style.

克孜尔千佛洞第38窟壁画 弥勒菩萨兜率天宫说法图
Frescoes in the No.38th cave: Maitreya preaching in Tushita Palace

石窟中的佛本生故事画在全国石窟中是首屈一指的。据不完全统计，克孜尔石窟佛本生故事画达70余种。此类题材有鸽王焚身济焚志、忍法龙慈心救毒蛇、尸毗王割肉贸鸽、熊王舍食活贫民、映子孝道父母、象王堕身济国王、须阇提太子割肉活父母、须达拏太子布施无极度、萨埵那舍身饲虎、金色王布施最后餐、四兽争相供焚志、独角仙人负女返城、恒伽达太子欲亡往阁世、猕猴以身作桥、幼象助狮搏莽、雄狮奋身救猿、鹦鹉灭火、鹿王代孕鹿烹、六牙白象献牙等等。其中“八国王争分舍利”是新疆石窟壁画中经常描绘的题材，多出现在洞窟后殿涅槃对面的龛壁上。这些生动感人的故事画多来源于民间传说。

克孜尔千佛洞第38窟壁画 波塞奇画佛
Frescoes in the No.38th cave: King Bosechi drawing a picture of Buddha

克孜尔千佛洞第38窟壁画 船师度佛过河缘（流失德国）
Frescoes in the No.38th cave: A karma story about a boatman taking Buddha across the river (now in Germany)

The Buddhist jataka paintings in the grottoes are second to none among the grottoes in China. According to incomplete statistics, there are more than 70 varieties of Buddhist jataka paintings in Kezier Thousand-Buddha Grottoes. The subjects include a dove king which burned itself to assist its generation, Dragon with a kind heart saved a viper, a king sliced off a piece of his flesh to save a dove, a bear king which sacrificed itself to save poor people, Yingzi's filial piety to parents, an elephant king which sacrificed itself to assist a king, Prince Sukuti cuts his flesh to save his parents, Prince Sudana gave limitless alm, Prince Sayina sacrificed himself to feed a tiger, Golden King gave alms for the last dinner, four animals offering to be burned as a sacrifice, immortal with a single horn carried a girl back to town, Prince Henchida was going to die to previous generation, macaque made a bridge of itself, a young elephant assisted a lion to attack a boa, a male lion vigorously saved an ape, parrots put out a fire, deer king did deer cook, six-ivory elephants offered their ivory, etc. Among them, the subject “eight kings strove to divide Buddhist relics” is frequently seen in the mural paintings in Xinjiang grottoes, mostly on shrine walls opposite nirvana in the back hall in grottoes. These vivid and touching story paintings mostly originated from folk legends.

克孜尔千佛洞第38窟壁画 锯陀兽剥皮救猎狮

Frescoes in the No.38th cave: Peeling the skin to save the hunting lions

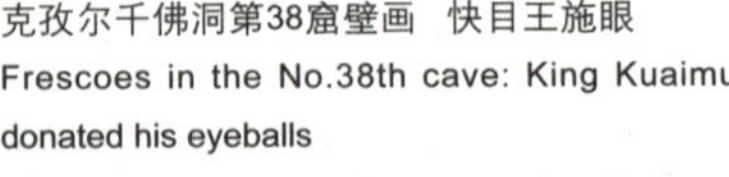

克孜尔千佛洞第38窟壁画 快目王施眼

Frescoes in the No.38th cave: King Kuaimu donated his eyeballs

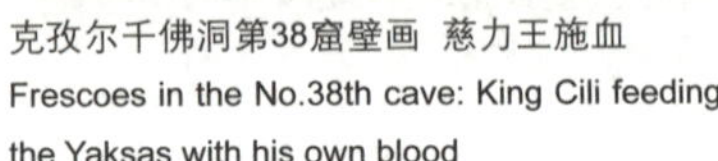

克孜尔千佛洞第38窟壁画 慈力王施血

Frescoes in the No.38th cave: King Cili feeding the Yaksas with his own blood

克孜尔千佛洞第38窟壁画 弥兰本生

Frescoes in the No.38th cave: Milinda Jataka

克孜尔千佛洞第38窟壁画
母鹿本生
Frescoes in the No. 38th cave: The doe Jataka.

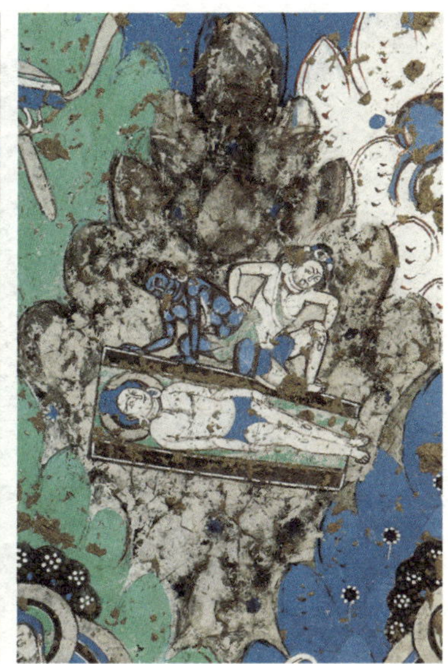

克孜尔千佛洞第38窟壁画 慕魄太子不言被埋
Frescoes in the No.38th cave: The mute Prince Mupo was buried.

克孜尔千佛洞第38窟壁画 婆罗门闻法舍身
Frescoes in the No.38th cave: Brahman sacrificed himself after hearing the preaching of Buddha

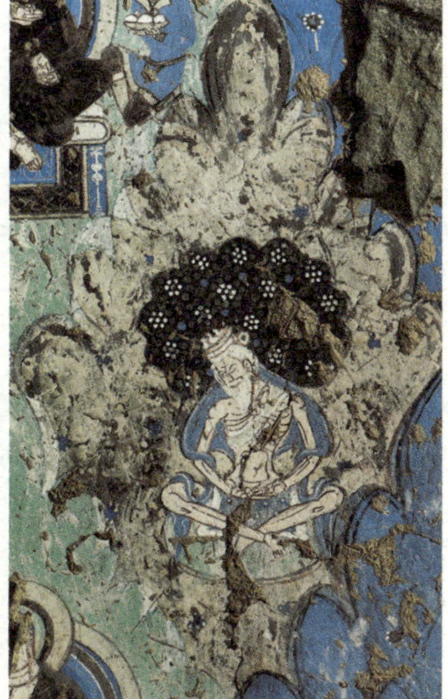

克孜尔千佛洞第38窟壁画 菩萨行慈不怖众生
Frescoes in the No.38th cave: Bodhisattva kindly shows compassion to the people.

克孜尔千佛洞第38窟壁画 萨缚燃臂引路
Frescoes in the No.38th cave: Safu burned his arm to illuminate the way.

克孜尔千佛洞第38窟壁画 树下观耕
Frescoes in the No.38th cave: Watching land cultivation under the tree

佛因缘故事

佛教常以事物相互间的关系来说明它们产生和变化的现象，其中事物产生或毁灭的主要条件叫做因，辅助条件叫做缘，合称因缘。

石窟的佛因缘故事种类较多，构图与布置部位多与佛本生故事相同。所不同的地方主要有两点：一是佛因缘故事画中的主角是佛，而佛本生故事画的主角则是菩萨，是人，甚至是动物，故事内容比较难以辨识和区分。二是佛因缘故事侧重表现佛的伟大神通力和众生对佛所做的种种供养。其画面多是中间为侧身而坐的佛，旁边安排一或两身有关人物。如克孜尔千佛洞175窟中的《梵志燃灯因缘》，说的是梵志在黑暗中用白毡布缠头，用火燃烧，以供众佛。又如《波塞奇因缘》，表现画佛左手托画钵，右手执画笔，前立一人执画布，佛操笔自画。在克孜尔178窟中还可见到《沙弥守戒自杀因缘》说一年少沙弥往长者家乞食，遇长者女爱慕，为保持清白而守戒自杀。另外在克孜尔224窟中还可见《须摩提女请佛因缘》，说一长者女招请佛及弟子至夫家，令全家皈依佛教等等。

Buddhist Karma Stories

Buddhism often explains the creation and changes of things by their mutual relations including the principal causes for the creation or destruction of things and the subsidiary causes, which compose the karma.

In the grottoes there are various karma stories and the composition and layout of paintings are mostly same as Buddhist jataka stories. There are two differences: first, the protagonist in Buddhist karma story paintings is Buddha while the protagonist in Buddhist jataka story paintings is Bodhisattva, people and animals and the story contents are hard to identify or differentiate. Second, Buddhist karma stories attach importance to showing the great superpower of Buddha and various provisions offered to Buddha by common people. In the paintings Buddha often sits on his side in the middle and one or two relevant figures are beside. For example, in No. 175 Grotto in Kezier Thousand-Buddha Grottoes the painting *Karma of Brahmacdarin* (Herectic Ascetic) *Lighting* tells that Brahmacdarin (Herectic Ascetic) wrapped his head with white felt in the darkness and burned it to offer sacrifice to all the Buddhas. *Bosechi Karma* expresses that a Painting Buddha held a painting bowl in his left hand and a paint brush in his right hand. A man stood before him and held a piece of canvas and the Buddha painted by himself. In No. 178 Kezier Grotto there is the painting *Karma for Buddhist Novice to Preserve Religious Discipline and Commit Suicide*. It tells that a young Buddhist novice begged for alms to an elder's family and encountered his daughter who loved the Buddhist novice. In order to preserve pure and religious disciplines, he committed suicide. In addition, in No. 224 Kezier Grotto there is the painting *Karma for a Sumoti Woman* Invited a Buddha. It tells that an elder's woman invited Buddha and his disciples to her husband's family and converted the whole family to Buddhism.

克孜尔千佛洞第123窟壁画 立佛

Frescoes in the No.123th cave: Standing Buddha

这些佛因缘故事壁画，各有不同的主题思想和艺术形式，其目的都是向众生灌输佛教思想。综观石窟佛因缘故事中的人物形象、衣冠服饰、社会生活等，充满了现实世界情景，脱离了佛陀的境界，从而具有浓郁的生活气息，再现了当时龟兹国的某些风貌。

佛传故事

佛传故事又叫做佛本行故事，是释迦牟尼一生中各阶段形象的综合。一般讲他诞生以后，王太子的生活，放弃太子身份而出家修道，成为所谓等正觉佛后的教化事迹，直至去世前后的生平故事。

克孜尔千佛洞第172窟壁画 日天问佛日月往行缘

Frescoes in the No.172th cave: The sun, the moon, the heaven and the Buddha- the Karma

克孜尔千佛洞第175窟壁画 无恼指鬘

Frescoes in the No.175th cave: Karma story about Wunao and the finger garland

克孜尔千佛洞第188窟壁画 菱格因缘故事壁画
Frescoes in the No.188th cave: Story about karma drawn in diamond pane

克孜尔千佛洞第69窟壁画 燃灯佛授记
Frescoes in the No.69th cave: Dipamkara making prediction of Buddhahood

These mural paintings about Buddhist karma stories have different subjects and artistic forms but the same motive: infuse common people with Buddhist thoughts. With a comprehensive view on the figures, clothes and caps and social life of the characters in Buddhist karma stories, they are full of scenes of the actual world and break away from the world of Buddha, so the flavor of life is strong and scenes of Kucha Kingdom at that time are reproduced.

Buddha Biography Stories

Buddha biography stories are also called Buddha stories of his line. They are the integration of Sakyamuni's images in different stages in his life. Usually speaking, after his birth as a prince, he abandoned his status as prince and became a monk to cultivate himself according to Buddhist doctrines. They tell the stories of his life after he became Zhengjue Buddha until his death.

克孜尔千佛洞第193窟壁画　龙王
Frescoes in the No.193th cave: The King of Dragon

克孜尔千佛洞第205窟壁画　焚棺图（流失德国）
Frescoes in the No.205th cave: Burning coffin (now in Germany)

克孜尔千佛洞第205窟壁画　龟兹国王和王后
Frescoes in the No.205th cave: The king and queen of ancient Kucha

龟兹地区的佛传故事画多在克孜尔石窟中描绘，主要有两类。一类描述佛的一生传记，主要布置在方形窟主室四壁，以连续方格画面，将佛从降诞到涅槃过程铺陈出来，犹如连环画形式。另一类着重讲佛成道后诸方说法教化的圣迹，即说法图，主要布置在中心柱窟和方形窟主室两侧壁，一格一画；有的是通壁绘几个说法图。在克孜尔石窟中，各种佛传故事题材就有60余种。

有关释迦牟尼的传记，起初并无系统的记载，后来，把经典中散记的传记集中、润色，就形成了佛传故事，由于不同时期所依经本不同，因而壁画中的佛传故事各有详略和侧重。石窟壁画中的佛传故事主要依据《佛本行集经》绘出。其中，突出了降魔成道和鹿野苑初转法轮的内容，主要布置在中心柱窟主室门上方和方形窟正壁等显要位置。此外，表现弥勒菩萨于兜率天宫说法的场面也不少，多布置在中心柱窟主室正上方，与正壁龛中佛相对。

Most of the Buddha biography stories in Kucha region were painted in Kezier grottoes. They include two types. One is about the biographies of Buddha and such paintings were mainly placed on the surrounding walls of major rooms in square grottoes. The course from Buddha's birth to his nirvana was narrated in consecutive square pictures, like strip pictures. The other is mainly about Buddha's holy deeds of visiting various places to educate others, i.e. the pictures of expounding Buddhist doctrines. They were mainly placed on the side walls of the center pillar grotto and the major rooms of square grottoes, one painting in a grid, and in some cases several pictures were painted on the same wall. In Kezier grottoes there are more than 60 varieties of subjects about Buddha biography stories.

There was no systematic record about the biography of Sakyamuni at the beginning. Later, the biographies scattered in sutras were gathered and embellished to form the Buddha biography stories. Depending on different sutras in different times, the Buddha biography stories in the mural paintings have different emphasis and details. The Buddha biography stories in the mural paintings in the grottoes were mainly painted according to *Life of Sakyamuni*. Among them, importance was attached to the contents such as subduing evil and becoming Buddha and turning the Buddhist wheel initially in Sarnath, which were mainly placed distinctive positions such as above the major door in the central pillar grotto and the central wall in square grottoes. In addition, there are many paintings about Maitreya expounding Buddhist doctrines in the Heavenly Palace, which were mainly placed on the central upside of the major rooms of center pillar grotto, opposite to Buddha in the shrine on the central wall.

克孜尔千佛洞第60窟壁画对雁联珠纹

Frescoes in the No.60th cave: Design of two wild gooses in opposite positions

克孜尔千佛洞第76窟壁画 出游四门（流失德国）

Frescoes in the No.76th cave: The excursions out of the four gates (now in Germany)

克孜尔千佛洞第76窟壁画 树下诞生（流失德国）

Frescoes in the No.76th cave: Birth under the tree (now in Germany)

在克孜尔千佛洞110窟中，左、右、中央三壁全部绘制佛传故事，每壁分上、中、下三层，共63幅，布局比较独特。在175窟中，只将佛传中某些重要情节描绘出来，如把“降魔”绘在南龛北内侧面上，把“降伏火龙”绘在南龛上面，又如在175窟后室左、右端壁上部绘出佛的“诞生”、“学步”、“出四门”等佛传题材，这样，就把释迦牟尼一生中诞生、降魔、说法、涅槃等主要事迹，在不同部分加以渲染，加强了佛教宣传效果。69窟主室门上方半圆形壁画，则是一幅鹿野苑说法图，场面之大，人物之多，实属罕见，表现了佛成道后，为五比丘说法之内容。118窟中有一幅《娱乐太子图》，表现了佛在做太子时，因看到世间烦恼，而想出家；其父王以宫女、歌舞感动他，希望他回心转意之内容。这幅说法图用象征的手法和独特的构图来揭示佛教中“禁欲”这一主题，表现得非常深刻。

In No. 110 Grotto in Kezier Thousand-Buddha Grottoes Buddha biography stories were painted on the left, right and central walls and each wall was divided into three layers, i.e. up, middle and down sides. There are 63 paintings placed in unique layout. In No. 175 Grotto, only some important themes in Buddha biography were painted. For example, “subduing evils” was painted on the northern interior of the southern shrine and “subduing fire dragon” was painted on the upper side of the southern shrine. In No. 175 Grotto such subjects as “birth”, “learning to walk” and “going out of four doors” were painted on the upper side of left and right walls in the back room. So Sakyamuni’s major deeds in his life such as birth, subduing evils, expounding Buddhist doctrines and nirvana were exaggerated in different places to strengthen the spreading effects of Buddhism. In No. 69 Grotto the mural painting in a semicircle above the major door is a painting about expounding Buddhist doctrines in Sarnath. Such a big scene and numerous figures were rarely seen. They described Buddha expounding Buddhist doctrines to five monks after he got the doctrines. In No. 118 Grotto there is a painting of *Amusing Prince*, describing that at the time of being a prince, Buddha wanted to become a monk at seeing the trouble in life. His father used maids and dancing and singing to move him and hoped he could change his views. This painting exposed profoundly the subject of “mortification” in Buddhism by means of symbolization and unique composition.

涅槃

涅槃原意是指火的熄灭或风的吹散。《杂阿含经》卷十八中说："贪欲永尽，嗔恚永尽，愚痴永尽，一切烦恼永尽，是名涅槃。"这就是说，作为人生的归宿亦即佛教最高理想则是涅槃。原始佛教认为涅槃是一种超越时空、超越经验、超越苦乐，不可思议，不可言传的实在，是一种"常乐我净"的理想境界。这使得信奉"无常、无乐、无我、不净"的小乘说教的僧侣们兴奋一时，信心徒增。这里的"常"指永恒，"乐"指幸福，"我"指自由，"净"指高洁。这样的宗教王国，对众生自然是有相当吸引力的。

新疆石窟中往往在甬道之后壁上出现涅槃像，如克孜尔17窟中可见，并有举哀菩萨弟子像。或者在后室之后壁前，凿出宽2.2米，长10米的石台，台上塑涅槃像，如克孜尔47窟中即是，可惜涅槃像已不存，但仍可见众比丘举哀图。

Nirvana

Originally nirvana refers to extinguishing of fire or blowing of wind. It is said in Volume 18 in *Samyutta Agama* (miscellaneous Agama) "greed, anger, foolery and all troubles came to end forever, which is called nirvana." It means that nirvana is the end-result of life and also the supreme ideal of Buddhism. Original Buddhism believed that nirvana surpassed space and time, experiences and bitterness and joy; it was an inconceivable and inexpressible actuality and was an ideal realm that "common people are happy and I am pure." This made monks who believed in Hinayana doctrines, "no permanence, no happiness, no freedom and no nobleness", increase their confidence. Such a religious kingdom was naturally attractive to common people.

Figures of nirvana often appear in the mural paintings behind walkways in Xinjiang grottoes such as No. 17 Grotto in Kezier, as well as statues of disciples of mourning Bodhisattva. Or before the back wall in the back rooms, a stone stage of 2.2 meters wide and 10 meters long was carved out and a nirvana statue was made on the stage, such as in No. 47 Kezier Grotto. It is a pit that the nirvana statue disappeared but there is still the painting of all monks going into mourning.

克孜尔千佛洞第76窟壁画　飞天（流失德国）
Frescoes in the No.76th cave: Fly Apsaras
(now in Germany)

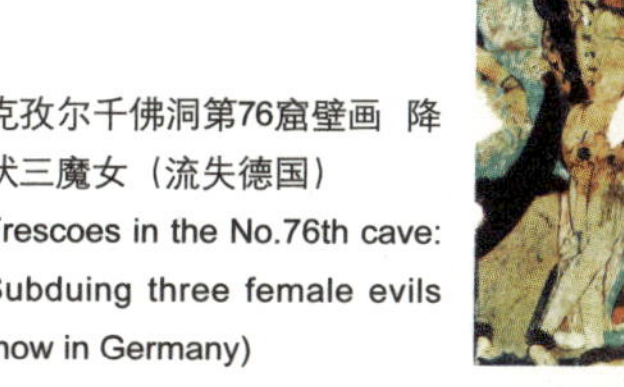

克孜尔千佛洞第76窟壁画　降伏三魔女（流失德国）
Frescoes in the No.76th cave: Subduing three female evils
(now in Germany)

克孜尔千佛洞第76窟壁画　降魔（流失德国）
Frescoes in the No.76th cave: Subduing evils
(now in Germany)

克孜尔千佛洞第104窟壁画 长老比丘在母胎六十年

Frescoes in the No. 104th cave: The Elder Bhiksu has been in the womb for 60 years.

克孜尔千佛洞第104窟壁画 四蛇喻

Frescoes in the No.104th cave: The metaphor of four snakes

克孜尔千佛洞第80窟壁画 降伏六师外道

Frescoes in the No.80th cave: Vanquishing the heretics

佛徒四众

佛徒四众，是指由“比丘”、“比丘尼”、“优婆塞”、“优婆夷”四部分人组成的释迦弟子。比丘，梵文Bhiksu的音译，意译为“乞士”，因以乞食为生而得名，指出家修行的男性佛教徒，俗称“和尚”。比丘尼，梵文Bhiksuni的音译，意译为“乞女”，指出家修行的女性佛教徒，俗称“尼姑”。优婆塞，梵文Upasaka的音译，意译为“近善男”，指信奉佛教而在家修行的男人，即“善男”，也叫做“居士”。优婆夷，梵文Upasika的音译，意译为“近善女”，指信奉佛教而在家修行的女人，即“信女”。所谓“善男信女”之成语即指后二者。

Four Groups of Buddhist Disciples

Four groups of Buddhist disciples refer to the disciples of Sakyamuni composed of four groups, i.e. “Bhiksu”, “Bhiksuni”, “Upasaka” and “Upasika”. Bhiksu, paraphrased as “men beggars” in Chinese as they lived on begging, refers to male Buddhist disciples who entered into religion and cultivated themselves, commonly called “monks”. Bhiksuni, paraphrased as “women beggars” in Chinese, refers to female Buddhist disciples who entered into religion and cultivated themselves, commonly called “nuns”. Upasaka, meaning “men seeking goodness” in Chinese, refers to men believing in Buddhism and cultivating themselves at home, i.e. “Buddhist laymen” or “lay Buddhists”. Upasika, meaning “women seeking goodness” in Chinese, refers to women believing in Buddhism and cultivating themselves at home, i.e. “Buddhist laywomen”.

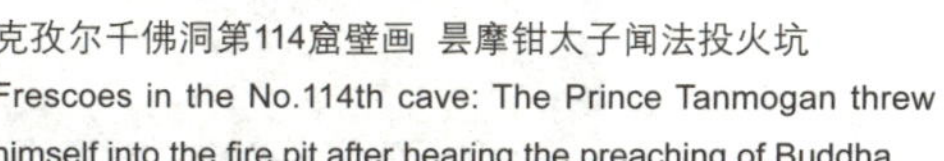

克孜尔千佛洞第114窟壁画 昙摩钳太子闻法投火坑
Frescoes in the No.114th cave: The Prince Tanmogan threw himself into the fire pit after hearing the preaching of Buddha.

克孜尔千佛洞第104窟壁画 供养人
Frescoes in the No.104th cave: The donors

克孜尔千佛洞第38窟壁画 天宫伎乐
Frescoes in the No.38th cave: performance in heavenly palace

天宫伎乐

石窟壁画中出现了许多或手持各种乐器或翩翩起舞的形象，虽然有的也是飞天形式，但也有许多是独立出现的，因为大都是佛国的歌舞表演，故称之为“天宫伎乐”。克孜尔38窟主室两壁绘满了天宫伎乐，均为两人一组，一人手持乐器，一人用手做舞姿。其中出现了排萧、五弦、阮咸、笛、凤首箜篌等乐器和各种舞姿。综观龟兹石窟壁画共出现了二十四种乐器，其中弦鸣乐器有五弦琵琶、三弦琵琶、四弦琵琶、四弦阮咸、三弦阮咸、曲颈四弦琵琶、坚箜篌、凤首箜篌、筝。气鸣乐器有排萧、洞萧。筚篥、双筚篥、笛、笙、锁纳、铜声、贝。膜鸣乐器有羯鼓、腰鼓、答腊鼓、都昙鼓、毛员鼓。体鸣乐器有铜钹等。演奏乐器形式中有飞天、供养菩萨，也有自奏自舞或乐器合奏，千姿百态，形形色色。

克孜尔千佛洞第171窟壁画 五通比丘论苦之本
Frescoes in the No. 171th cave: Wutong Bhiksu explaining the root of bitterness

Performance in Heavenly Palace

In the mural paintings in the grottoes there are many figures holding various musical instruments or dancing elegantly. Some are in form of flying goddess and many appeared independently. As most of them expressed the performance of singing and dancing in Buddhist state, they are called “performance in heavenly palace”. In No. 38 Kezier Grotto the paintings about performance in heavenly palace were painted on the two walls of the major room. Two performers in a team, one holding musical instruments and the other dancing with hand motions. There appear such musical instruments as xiao pipes, five-string, ruanxian (an ancient stringed musical instrument), flute and harp with phoenix head (an ancient plucked stringed instrument) and various dancing postures. With a comprehensive view of the grotto mural paintings in Kucha, 24 kinds of musical instruments appear. The stringed instruments include five-stringed pipa, three-stringed pipa, four-stringed pipa, four-stringed ruanxian, three-stringed ruanxian, four-stringed pipa with bent neck, harp, harp with phoenix head and zither. Wind instruments include xiao and dong pipes, bili, double bili, flute, sheng, suona, tongsheng, and bei. Musical instruments include jie drum, waistdrum, dala drum, duyun drum and maoyuan drum as well as bronze cymbals. The forms of playing musical instruments include flying goddess, offering sacrifice to Bodhisattva, playing and dancing by the same person or instrumental ensemble. They are in various and colorful postures.

鸠摩罗什

佛教中三大翻译家之一的鸠摩罗什就出生在这里，今天的克孜尔千佛洞前，就有鸠摩罗什的青铜像。鸠摩罗什大师像坐落在高1.05米的莲花形花岗岩石座上。乍见大师像，大师虔诚宁静的态度忽地让人心若止水，那微闭的双目、微垂的头颅似乎都只是为佛而来。在库车纯净蔚蓝的天空映衬下，罗什大师的黑色铜像更显虔诚神秘，罗什大师就是龟兹文化的精髓。

鸠摩罗什大师像
Statue of Master Kumarajiva

克孜尔石窟出土 泥塑彩绘菩萨头像
Unearthed in Kezier Grottoes: Standing Buddha (clay sculpture with colored drawings)

克孜尔石窟出土
木板画 立佛像（左）
Unearthed in Kezier Grottoes: Standing Buddha (wooden board painting) (left)

克孜尔石窟出土（右）
木板画 双头立佛像
Unearthed in Kezier Grottoes: Standing two head Buddha (wooden board painting) (rigth)

Kumaralabdha

Kumaralabdha, one of the three great translators in Buddhism, was born here. Before the present-day Kezier Thousand-Buddha Grottoes there is the bronze statue of Kumaralabdha on a lotus-shaped granite foundation of 1.05 meters high. With a glance at the master's statue, the devotion and calm attitude of the master makes people suddenly become calm like still water, and his slightly-closed eyes and slightly-drooped head seem like being born for Buddha. Set off by the pure and blue sky in Kuche, the dark bronze statue of Master Kumarajiva looks more devotional and mysterious and he is the elite of Kucha culture.

克孜尔千佛洞第188窟壁画 幡供养
Frescoes in the No.188th cave: Contribution with flag

克孜尔千佛洞第188窟壁画 花环供养
Frescoes in the No.188th cave: contribution with garland

克孜尔千佛洞第188窟壁画 净居天洗佛
Frescoes in the No.188th cave: Washing Buddha in pure-dwelling heavens

鸠摩罗什大师于公元344年生于龟兹，其父曾为天竺某国宰相，因国破侨居龟兹，后龟兹王赐其与王妹成婚。鸠摩罗什7岁时随母亲在本地出家，9岁学小乘佛教，后遇大乘教名僧影响，弃小乘而归大乘。少年罗什聪慧颖悟，远近闻名，后龟兹王尊其为国师。曾有记载说西域诸王每次来听罗什讲经，都是长列座侧，让罗什踩背而登。前秦大将军吕光破龟兹，征服西域三十余国，得鸠摩罗什与2万峰骆驼，鸠摩罗什被迎往凉州，在凉州呆了近20年，继续弘扬佛法。公元401年，又被迎往长安，尊为国师，在草堂寺译经讲法，与其弟子共译出佛经74部384卷，主要有《摩诃般若波罗蜜经》、《中论》、《妙法莲花经》等，对中国佛教的三论宗、天台宗、成实宗、净土宗影响巨大。公元409年，大师辞世，终年七十岁，临终时大师留下遗言，将他的舌头葬于姑藏以证其曾说的“要是没有违背意愿，死后火化时舌头不烂。”今天的甘肃武威北大街西侧罗什寺塔就是埋葬他“不烂舌头”的地方。

Master Kumaralabdha was born in 344 in Kucha. His father was prime minister of a state in India. As his state was conquered, he moved to Kucha and later the King of Kucha allowed him to marry his daughter. At the age of 7 Kumaralabdha entered into religion with his mother in his hometown. At 9 he studied Hinayana and later due to effect by a famous monk of Mahayana, he abandoned Hinayana and converted to Mahayana. The young Kumarajiva was very intelligent and famous far and near. Later the King of Kucha respected him as state master. There are records that every time kings in the western region came to listen to lectures by Kumarajiva they sat in lines and let Kumarajiva ascend on their backs General Lu Guang of the former Qing Dynasty attacked Kucha, conquered about thirty states in the western region, and received Kumaralabdha and 20,000 camels. Kumaralabdha was welcomed to Liangzhou, and lived in Liangzhou for almost 20 years, continuing to carry forward the doctrines of Buddhism. In 401, Kumaralabdha was welcomed to Chang'an and respected as state master. Kumaralabdha translated sutras and preached the doctrines of Buddhism in Caotang Temple. He translated 74 sections, 384 volumes of sutras with his disciples, mainly including *All-Embracing Sutra*, *The Middle Way*, and *Sutra of the Lotus*, which had a great effect on the San-lun School (Three-Treatiese School), Tendai School, Ch'eng-shih School and (Satyasiddhi-sastra School) Ching-t'u Sect (Sukhavati Sect) of Chinese Buddhism. In 409, the master passed away when he was seventy years old. On his deathbed, the master said, his tongue would be buried in Guzang to prove the words he had said, "if not violating his will, his tongue would be intact when his body was cremated after his death." Today, the tower of Kumarajiva Temple in the west on the north avenue of Wuwei, Gansu Province is the place where "the intact tongue" was buried.

克孜尔千佛洞第189窟壁画 舍卫城神变

Frescoes in the No.189th cave: The magical change in Sravasti

千泪泉
Spring of Thousand Tears

千泪泉

千泪泉是克孜尔千佛洞所在地的一处奇异景观，周围为草木葱郁的幽谷，谷底端头，一道石壁高耸，呈半弯状。从高达百丈布满苔藓峭壁间，泉滴无数，落聚成潭，又汩汩流出谷外，见者无不称奇。民间传说：古龟兹国公主与一贫家青年相爱而信誓旦旦。国王认为有辱门风，蓄意阻难，命令这个青年在悬崖上凿出千座洞窟，否则，非但不许娶公主为妻，而且还要严加惩处。那青年毅然上山，拼尽全力，开凿洞窟。当他凿出 999个洞窟时，便力竭身亡。公主闻讯赶来，抱尸痛哭了三天三夜，终于泪尽气绝。这纯真的生死之恋，感动得峭壁岩石为之纷纷垂泪，历千年而不止，故得名“千泪泉”。

Thousand-Tear Spring

Thousand-Tear Spring is a fantastic scene at the location of Kezier Thousand-Buddha Grottoes. Luxurious green grass and trees encircle the spring in the secluded valley. At the end of the valley a cliff rises up in the shape of semi-circle. Countless drops of spring water fall down from the, moss covered, hundreds-of-meters high cliff coming together to form a pool and then runs out of the valley. Anyone seeing it will feel it is fantastic. There is a folk legend: a princess of the ancient Kucha State fell in love with a poor young man and they vowed their love solemnly. The King thought she was a shame to the family and intended to obstruct them. He ordered the young man to carve out a thousand grottoes on the cliff, or else he could not marry the princess and would receive severe punishment. The young man went up to the mountain resolutely and exhausted his efforts to carve out grottoes. Upon carving out the No. 999 grotto, he died of exhaustion. The princess hurried to see him at hearing the news. She carried the body, cried her eyes out for three days and nights and at last died with exhaustion of tears. This pure love of life and death moved cliff and rocks to tear for a thousand years, hence the “Thousand-Tear Spring”.

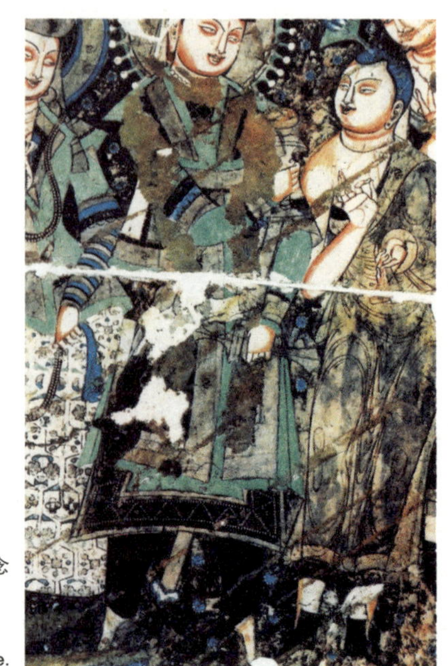

克孜尔千佛洞第205窟壁画　比丘悬念释解女尸缘
Frescoes in the No. 205th cave: Bhiksu solved the mystery over a woman corpse.

艾提尕尔清真寺

ETIGAR MOSQUE

位于喀什市中心的艾提尕尔清真寺

The Etigar Mosque is located in the center of Kashgar city

位于喀什市中心的艾提尕尔清真寺，是中国维吾尔族创建的历史瑰宝之一。它以其悠久的历史，雄伟的建筑和绚丽的色彩等特点，闻名于中外。它在中亚地区与布哈拉、撒马尔罕等地的著名大清真寺一样，受到广大穆斯林的瞩目。

The Etigar Mosque, located in the center of Kashgar City in Xinjiang Uygur Autonomous Region, is one of the important historical heritages of the Uygur people. It is well known at home and abroad because of its long history, grand construction and beautiful color. Like the famous mosques in Bukhara and Samarkand, the Etigar Mosque attracts attention from numerous Muslims.

艾提尕尔清真寺正门门厅

The lobby of the Etigar Mosque

“艾提尕尔”一词，是新疆信仰伊斯兰教的穆斯林对做礼拜的大清真寺的通称。也有人把它按阿拉伯语的“尔德”（变音为“艾提”，意思是节日）和波斯语的“尕尔”（意思是广场），解释为“节日场所”，但此种说法并不完全正确。固然在伊斯兰的各种节日里，清真寺是主要的活动场所，而在平时，穆斯林们也同样在这里进行日常的宗教活动。

The word “Etigar” refers to the mosques in which the Muslims in Xinjiang Uygur Autonomous Region gather to conduct religious services. Some people argue that “Etigar” means a “Festival Plaza”, because the inflexion of “eti” in Arabic means “festival” and “gar” in Persian means “Plaza”. However, this is not completely right. The mosque is not only a main place for celebrating Islamic festivals, but also a place for Muslims to conduct regular religious activities.

艾提尕尔清真寺正门门楼
The gate tower of the main entrance to the Etigar Mosque

艾提尕尔清真寺礼拜厅阿訇讲经处
The place where imams make the preaching at the prayer hall of the Etigar Mosque

艾提尕尔清真寺是新疆自治区的重点文物保护单位。历年来，人民政府曾多次拨专款进行维修。1981年，又对艾提尕尔清真寺做了全面整修，使其焕然一新，以崭新、雄伟、庄重的面貌呈现在人们面前。

The Etigar Mosque is a key historical relic protection unit in Xinjiang Uygur Autonomous Region. The government has appropriated special funds for maintaining the Mosque many times over the years. The Mosque was fully renovated in 1981. Thus a grand, solemn and new Etigar Mosque appeared.

节日礼拜盛况的艾提尕尔广场
The Etigar Square when people are praying in the Festival

艾提尕尔清真寺面积达16800平方米，为新疆第一大清真寺，它由礼拜堂、教经堂、门楼和其他一些附属建筑物组成。大门高4.7米，大门楼高12米。门楼两边，各竖一座造型别致的圆柱形塔楼，高18米。塔顶端各有一召唤楼，楼顶立有一弯月。

The Etigar Mosque, covering an area of 16,800 square meters, is the largest mosque in Xinjiang. It consists of the Hall for worshiping, the Doctrine-Teaching Hall, the Gate Tower (square edifice of the gate) and other auxiliary structures. The gate is 4.7 meters high and the Gate Tower is 12 meters high. Each of the two sides of the Gate Tower is an 18-meter- high exquisite column structure. On top of each column stands a minaret with a meniscus (a minaret is, in Islamic religious architecture, the tower from which the faithful are called to prayer five times each day by a muezzin.).

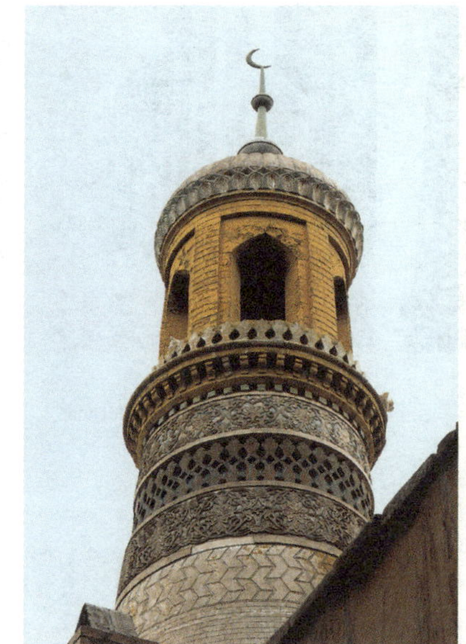

艾提尕尔清真寺宣礼塔
The Minaret at the Etigar Mosque

召唤阁
The Attic

艾提尕尔清真寺正门牌匾
The sign at the main entrance of the Etigar Mosque

艾提尕尔清真寺礼拜长廊顶棚上的图案
The ceiling decoration of the long corridor for prayer at the Etigar Mosque

艾提尕尔清真寺礼拜大殿
The prayer hall in the Etigar Mosque

重大礼拜活动时，艾提尕尔清真寺礼拜大殿内主持宣讲经义的讲座
The seat at the prayer hall, where imam sits and makes the preaching during important prayer activities

窗饰 Window decoration

大门 Door

门楼后面，是一个大拱北孜，其顶端也托着一座小尖塔，塔尖也有一弯黄铜做的新月。门楼、大门、尖塔、拱北孜组成一座雄伟的伊斯兰风格的典型建筑，令人肃然起敬。

Behind the Gate Tower is an entry arch with a small minaret on the top. There is also a brass meniscus on the top of the minaret. The Gate Tower, gate, minaret and entry arch form a typical Islamic grand and solemn mosque.

艾提尕尔清真寺内显示世界一些主要宗教圣地时间的时钟

In the Etigar Mosque, clocks shows the local time of the major holy land in the world

各种装饰墙花

Various wall decorations

进入寺门，是一个八角形的穿厅，左右两边均有甬道可进入寺内庭院。庭院面积有1公顷多，北半部有两个并列的大水池，南北两侧各有一排共36间教经堂，供阿訇讲经之用。院内池水碧绿，白杨参天，桑榆繁茂，显得格外幽静。礼拜堂高出地面1.5米，建在一个2660平方米的平台上。礼拜殿平面呈长方形，140根高达7米的绿色雕花木柱，支撑着白色的密肋天棚。天棚为木质藻井，彩绘各色图案。礼拜殿又可分为正殿和侧殿。正殿是密闭式长方形建筑．其后墙有一神龛，名为“米赫拉卜”，这就是穆斯林们进行礼拜时的正式“朝向”。龛旁置有一座木制雕花的宣讲台，台旁置一权杖。在节日和大礼拜时，大毛拉就站在台上宣讲《古兰经》。

Behind the portal is an octagonal hallway with two paved paths on the both sides. leading to the courtyard. The courtyard covers an area of one hectare, with two large parallel pools in the north. There are 36 Doctrine-Teaching Halls for imams to preach on both the south and north sides of the courtyard. There is a pond with rippling green jade water enclosed by flourishing poplar trees reaching toward the sky, as well as vigorous pines. It endows the mosque with a quiet elegance. The Hall for worshiping, rising 1.5 meters above the ground, is on a 2,660-square meter platform. The layout of the Hall is a rectangle. The white ribbed ceiling of this hall is supported by 140 sculptured wooden columns. Each column is seven meters high and painted green. The ceiling is a wooden coffered-ceiling with colorful painting patterns. The Hall for worshiping comprises an inner hall (main hall) and an outer hall. The enclosed main hall is a rectangle in shape. In the back wall in the main hall, there is a mihrab, a niche in the mosque indicating the direction of prayer (i.e. towards Mecca). Beside the mihrab sits a sculptured wooden minbar. A crosier is beside the minbar. During service and festivals, the grand Mullah stands on the minbar to preach the *Koran*.

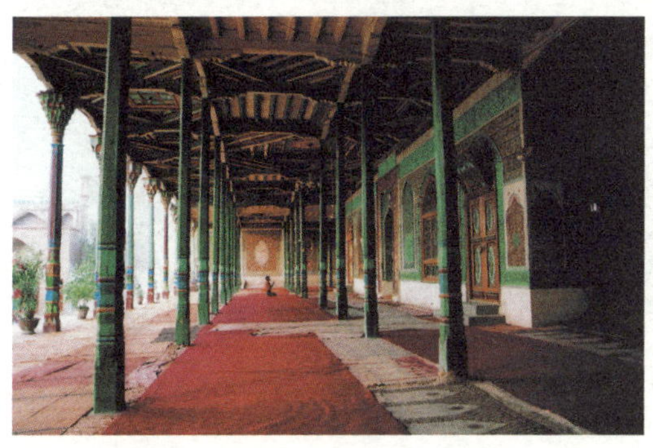

艾提尕尔清真寺院内长廊

The long corridor in the yard of the Etigar Mosque

在殿堂内外的地面上，铺有专供教民跪拜祈祷之用的地毯、绒毯、布单或苇席。平时做礼拜时，寺内教民可达2000～3000人，“主麻日”可达6000–7000人，重要节日有3万人以上，场面很大。这天清真寺内处处都跪着做礼拜的人，有时寺外的广场上也跪满了穆斯林。

Carpets, soft nap blankets, cloth sheets or reed mats are laid on the ground outside and inside the hall for praying. During the regular service, the Mosque can house 2,000-3,000 worshipers, and on the Jumah it can accommodate 6,000-7,000 worshippers. On important Islamic festivals it can hold as many as 30,000. On such a day, the Mosque will be full of kneeling worshippers. Sometimes, the square in front of the Mosque is also full of worshipers.

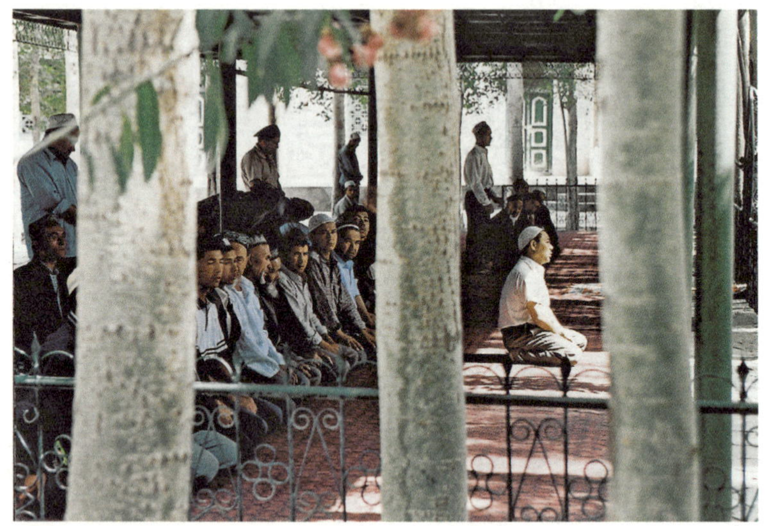

艾提尕尔清真寺内做礼拜的穆斯林
The Muslims are praying in the Etigar Mosque

艾提尕尔清真寺院内长廊中做礼拜的穆斯林
The Muslims are praying at the long corridor of the Etigar Mosque

外国游客在艾提尕尔清真寺
Foreign visitors at the Etigar Mosque

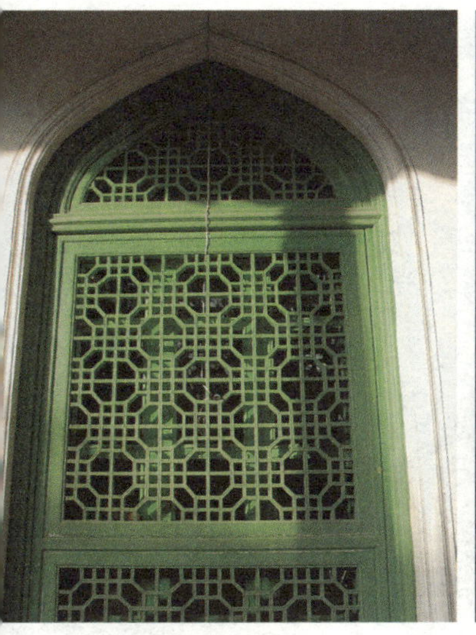

正殿的花窗
Window grill at the main hall

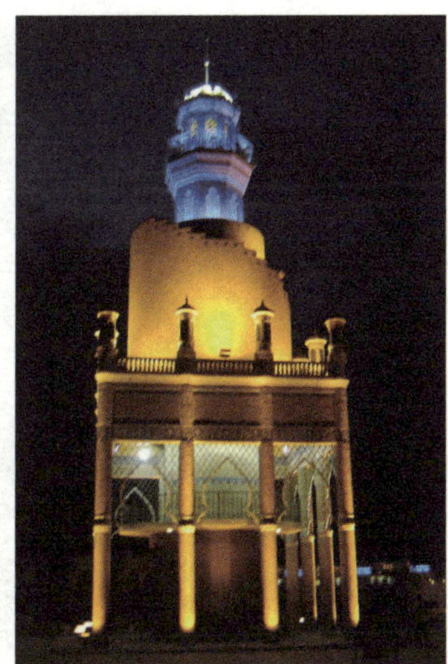

广场夜景
The night view of the square

鹅舞
Goose dance

艾提尕尔清真寺，已在喀什市中心雄立500多年了。据文献记载，早期的艾提尕尔清真寺，规模并不大，当时只是一座不起眼的小清真寺，公元1442年由喀什王沙克色孜·米扎尔的后裔所建。这个地方原来安葬着喀什噶尔的著名人物，如喀什王沙克色孜·米尔扎及其亲属、察合台后裔莎车王赛义德汗之弟米尔扎·艾则孜外里苏丹等。

The Etigar Mosque, located in the heart of Kashgar City, boasts a history of over 500 years. According to literature, the original Etigar Mosque was built in 1442 as a very small structure. It was built by the descendants of Shakesimirzha, the ruler of Kashgar. This place was originally a cemetery for Shakesimirzha and his family, as well as other renowned personalities like Mizar Achizwali Sodan, the brother of Sache Prince Sayd Khan, descendant of Chagatai Khan.

艾提尕尔清真寺正门外的圆形台阶
Round steps outside the main entrance of the Etigar Mosque

夜幕中的艾提尕尔清真寺
The Etigar Mosque in the evening

艾提尕尔清真寺内寺院工作人员居住的小院
The small courtyard for the staff in the Etigar Mosque

艾提尕尔清真寺门楼顶上响起欢快鼓乐，向人们昭示着节日的来临
The joyful drumbeats coming from the top of the Mosque's gate tower is the herald of the festival

公元 1537年，乌布里哈德尔·米扎尔阿尔伯克，为纪念葬于此地的叔父米尔扎·艾则孜外里，将原有的小寺扩大为能做主麻聚礼（每周的主麻日礼拜）的大寺。

The small mosque was enlarged to hold Jumah Prayer in 1537 by Woboli Hadar Mizar Arbok to monumentalize his uncle Mizar Achizwali Sodan.

古尔邦节里艾提尕尔清真寺门楼上的鼓乐手
The band at the gate tower of the Etigar Mosque in Corban Festival

节日的艾提尕尔清真寺外景
The exterior of the Etigar Mosque in festival time

艾提尕尔清真寺前欢乐的孩子们
The happy children in front of the Etigar Mosque

古尔邦节中在艾提尕尔广场跳舞的维吾尔族群众
Uighur people are dancing at the Etigar Square during the Corban Festival

阿訇的帽子
The prayer caps of imams

2006年古尔邦节期间穆斯林群众做礼拜的盛况
The significant view of prayer by Muslims during the Corban Festival in 2006

18世纪后期，有位叫古丽热拉的有钱妇女，在去巴基斯坦途中病逝于喀什。死前留下遗嘱，将遗产用来修建一座清真寺，就是后来的艾提尕尔清真寺的前身，当时规模也不大，寺院周围仍然是一片坟地。此后，艾提尕尔清真寺又进行了多次扩建。

In the late 18th century, a rich woman named Golirara became sick and died in Kashgar when she was on the way to Pakistan. She made a will before her death. She decided to donate her fortune to build a mosque and thus the Etigar Mosque which was not very big then was renovated and enlarged again. Around the mosque was still a cemetery. Several later renovations and enlargements followed.

1872年，艾提尕尔清真寺又大修一次，成了现在这样的规模。这次修建，把大寺分成2个部分：东面是清真寺，西面是教经堂。教经堂有供400名学生居住和学习的96个房间，同时还修建了可容100人洗澡的蒸气浴室，供400人取暖的暖室，增辟了4个人工水池。

In 1872, the Etigar Mosque was renovated fully again to the current scale and style. After renovation, the Mosque was divided into two parts. The east part is the mosque, and in the west are the Doctrine-Teaching Halls, with 96 rooms housing 400 Muslim students for dwelling and studying. A steam bath accommodating 100 people, and a heated room large enough to hold 400 people, as well as four man-made ponds were also added.

骆驼舞
Camel dance

艾提尕尔清真寺院墙外侧的商业店铺
Shops outside the walls of the Etigar Mosque

艾提尕尔广场上的和平鸽　Pigeons at the Etigar Square

经过历次修建扩大，不仅房间增多，设施增加，还广植树木花草，使清真寺环境更加幽静清新，它不仅是穆斯林们进行宗教活动的场所，而且成了喀什城内一个景色宜人的旅游圣地。

After several renovations and enlargements, the Etigar Mosque added more rooms and facilities. By planting more trees and grasses, the Mosque came to enjoy a tranquil environment and fresh air. It is not only a religious activity center but also a picturesque tourist attraction in Kashgar City.

艾提尕尔清真寺外的广场平时也是人们休闲娱乐的场所
The square outside the Etigar Mosque serves as an entertainment place as well

清真寺门前的儿童
The children in front of the Mosque

The Etigar Mosque is stands among crisscrossing streets and roads where you can find numerous shops. Shops featuring sheet iron cabinets and wood cabinets in styles which are peculiar to the Uygur people, line the streets. The bustling crowd and numerous shops demonstrate vigorous business opportunities. There is a poetic and picturesque look both inside and outside the Mosque. Standing through a long history, the Etigar Mosque and the clock tower on the Etigar Plaza add radiance to each other, forming a harmonious view. Tourists are always become engrossed in it.

古尔邦节前夕的喀什艾提尕尔广场
The Etigar Square before the Corban Festival

艾提尕尔清真寺两边的侧门外街衢纵横，店铺林立。维吾尔人特有的“铁皮柜”、“木柜式”等店铺沿街排列，人们熙熙攘攘，遍布的货摊满蕴勃勃商机，寺门内外如诗如画。尽管岁月悠悠，但艾提尕尔清真寺与艾提尕尔广场的时钟塔交相辉映，统一和谐的格局，仍令游人叹为观止。

穿着艾德莱斯绸的少女

The young girls in Etles silk

艾提尕尔清真寺里通向礼拜大殿的小路

The lane to the prayer hall of the Etigar Mosque

每当节日来临，艾提尕尔清真寺门前万头攒动，人声鼎沸。寺门顶部的平台上，唢呐吹得特别的嘹亮，鼓声响彻天空，方圆数里也能听见。尤其是古尔邦节，（即“宰牲节”），是维吾尔族诸多节日中最为隆重、热闹的重大节日。节日这天凌晨，穆斯林们早已将节日的盛装穿戴停当，坐家静心等待召唤，当听到从远处传来阿訇的呼唤声，纷纷向艾提尕尔广场涌来。此刻，艾提尕尔广场内外如潮水般汹涌，广场的每个角落都跪遍了穆斯林，秩序井然而谦让。礼拜开始，只隐隐约约听到领诵经文的阿訇的祷告声，广场上鸦雀无声，穆斯林们虔诚地祈祷着。礼毕，人们不分老少，便在清真寺门前跳起粗犷热烈的萨玛舞，舞者千姿百态，连跳3天，始终充满着喜庆热烈的节日气氛。

The front of the Etigar Mosque always sees crowds of people when it comes to the festivals. On the flat roof of the Mosque, people play the suona horn (a woodwind instrument) loudly and clearly; and they beat drums so heavily that people can hear the sound for miles around. In particular, the Id al-Kurban Festival (Eid al-Adha) is the most ceremonious and popular festival for the Uygur people. In the early morning of the festival, Muslims are all well dressed. They sit in their home calmly, just waiting for the summons of the imam. When the voice begins calling from far away, people surge to the Etigar Plaza. Almost everywhere you can see the Muslims kneeling for prayers. Despite the large number of people, they are orderly and treat each other with courtesy. When the worship begins, you will feel a silent and solemn atmosphere, only hearing the voice of prayer. After the ceremony, people no matter old or young dance the Sama dance rustically and ardently. The gestures of the dancers vary a lot. They keep dancing for three days, brimming with a festive atmosphere.

古尔邦节期间广场上的小吃摊
The snack stands at the square during the Corban Festival

喀什巴扎
The bazaar in Kashgar

提示：（1）游客进寺时要脱鞋。女性旅行者在有关部门和旅行社的协调和帮助下，取得寺方同意方可进寺参观，只是女游客不得穿着过于暴露。（2）如果想拍摄穆斯林礼拜的场面，一定要事先征得寺内阿訇（主持）的同意，而且不能站在朝拜人群的前方和侧面拍摄。（3）在清真寺里还有些应该注意遵守的当地习俗，如不能从做礼拜的人面前走过，更不能踩礼拜地毯，别人做礼拜时不能喧闹，诵读祈祷经文时不能说话等等。（4）每年“古尔邦”节的时候，场面最为宏大，人数最多的时候高达10万人，一定要在早晨7:00之前赶到。

Tips: (1) Tourists must take off their shoes before entering the Mosque. Female tourists can visit the Mosque only when they get permission of the Mosque with the coordination and assistance of relevant departments and tourist agencies. (2) If they want to photograph the Muslim worship, they must get the approval of the imam beforehand. Also it is not permitted to stand in front or on the side of the crowd that is worshiping. (3) Tourists must observe the local customs when they are in the Mosque. For example, they can't walk in front of the people that are worshiping; especially, they can't step on the carpets used for worshiping; they must keep silent when others are worshiping and chanting prayers. (4) Do remember to arrive there before 7:00 during the Corban Festival when the maximum participants may amount to 100,000.

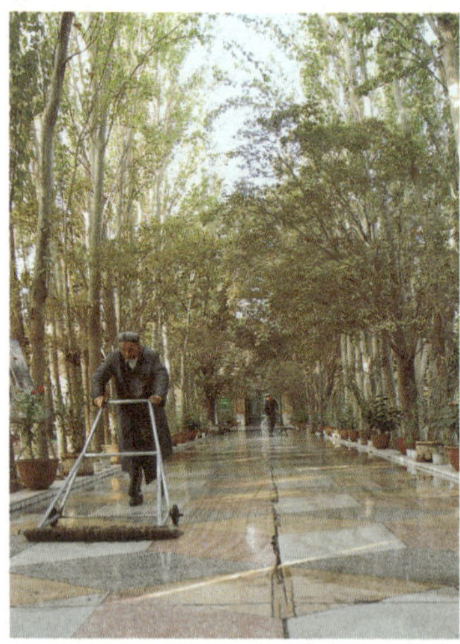

清真寺院内

The interior of the Mosque

艾提尕尔清真寺外

The exterior of the Etigar Mosque

艾提尕尔清真寺外的喀什老城区

The old town of Kashgar outside the Etigar Mosque

喀什小巷中的维吾尔族庭院

Uighur courtyard in the alley of Kashgar

喀什小巷
Alley in Kashgar

喀什小巷中绣花帽的维吾尔族妇女
The Uighur women embroidering cap in the alley of Kashgar

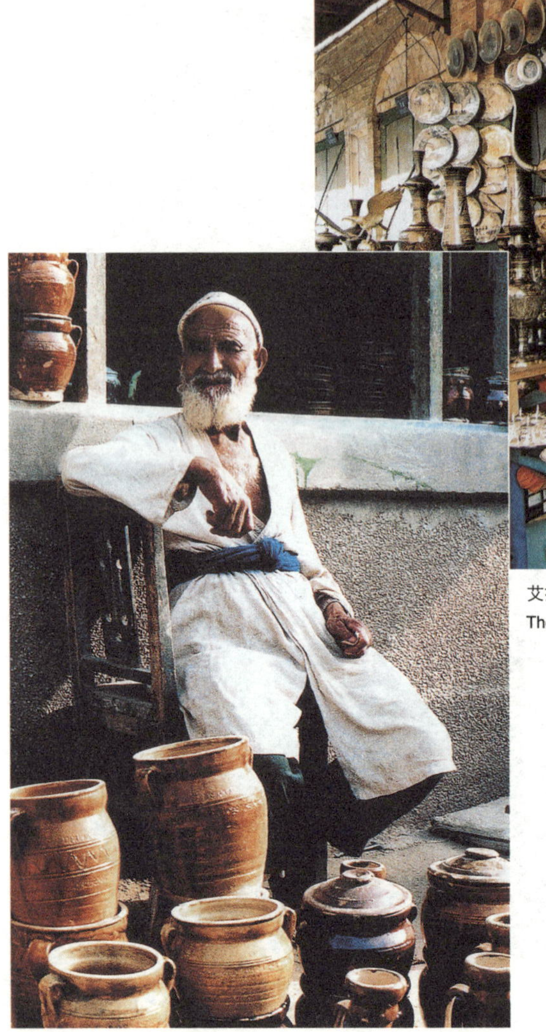

艾提尕尔清真寺院墙外侧的销售工艺品的店铺

The handicraft shops outside the walls of the Etigar Mosque

坎儿井

KAREZ

阿勒泰市
塔城市
克拉玛依市
博乐市
昌吉市
伊宁市
乌鲁木齐市
坎儿井
吐鲁番市
哈密市
库尔勒市
阿克苏市
阿图什市
喀什市
和田市

天山下的坎儿井
Karez at the foot of the Tianshan Mountain

“坎儿井”并不是井，而是在地表下开挖的一种奇特的引水渠道。在新疆的吐鲁番、鄯善县、托克逊县、哈密市都有坎儿井。全新疆共有坎儿井1600多条，以吐鲁番为最多，共有1044条，总长3000千米。吐鲁番地区的坎儿井最长的达30千米，最短的通常也有3千米左右。

A Karez is not a well but a particular kind of canal for drawing water. They can be found in Turpan, Shanshan County, Toksun County, and Hami City in Xinjiang province. Across Xinjiang, there are more than 1,600 karezes and most of them are in Turpan where the number is 1,044 and the total length is 3,000 km. The longest karez in Turpan is 30 km and the shortest one is about 3 km.

沿着火焰山流淌的明渠
Ground canals along the Flaming Mountain

吐鲁番盆地四周环山，山岭靠盆地的内缘是一圈戈壁砾石带，再向里便是绿洲带了。绿洲带中心是中国最低的湖泊艾丁湖，它的海拔为-154米。从北部的博格达山脚下到艾丁湖，仅60千米远，相差高度却有1400多米。这里地下水位的坡降和地面坡降相差无几，使吐鲁番形成了一个径流不能外泄的盆地。博格达山南坡共有现代冰川183条。面积122.37平方千米；西部的喀拉乌成山阿拉沟北岸有现代冰川42条，面积17.58平方千米。春季雪融，水从山顶直泻而下。夏季由于山高，拦截了高空水气，常形成山区地带暴雨或大雨。这里山地地面植被稀少，大多为裸露的基岩，因此雨水在地表很快形成径流，向盆地中心输送。进入戈壁砾石带后，由于砾石透水性极强，不少河流有50%的水流人地下，有的甚至全部渗人地下。这样就在盆地北、西边缘上形成了一个巨大的潜水带。正是这丰富的地下水和地形的坡度，成为挖掘坎儿井的重要条件。

The Turpan Basin is surrounded by mountains. From the edge of the mountains to the Basin is desert and in the middle is the oasis. At the center of the oasis is the lowest lake in China, Aiting Lake whose altitude is -154 meters. The distance from the foot of Bogada Mountain in the north to Aiting Lake is only 60 km but the difference between their altitudes is more than 1,400 meters. The fall of the underground water is almost the same as that of the ground which makes Turpan become a basin where water ways cannot run out. On the southern slope of Bogada Mountain there are 183 modern glaciers covering an area of 122.37 square km. To the west on the northern bank of the Alagou in the Kalawucheng Mountains there are 42 modern glaciers covering an area of 17.58 square km. In spring when the snow thaws the water runs down directly from the mountains into the lake. In the summer due to the high mountains the rain clouds are intercepted which results in heavy rain in the mountains. Most of the mountains are exposed bedrock and ground plants in are very rare so the rain water soon forms streams on the ground which run to the center of the basin. After running into the desert zone and due to the strong permeability of the gravel, 50 percent of the water runs underground. The water of some of the rivers even runs totally underground. Over a period of time a huge underground water zone came into being at the northern and western edges of the basin. The underground water and the slope of the land combine to give the ideal conditions for digging out karezes.

吐鲁番坎儿井
Karez in Turpan

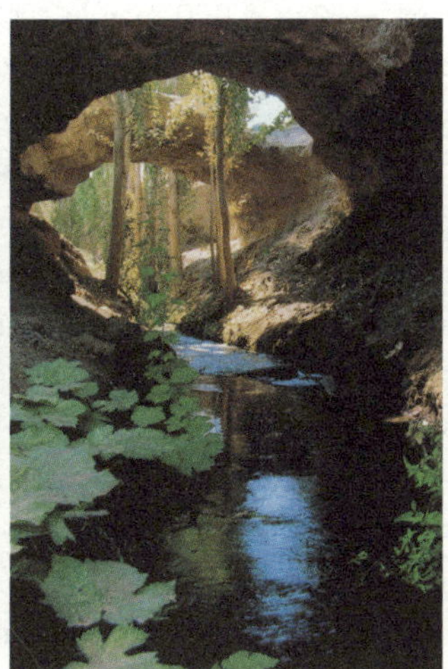

坎儿井暗渠
Underground canals of karez

坎儿井
Karez

吐鲁番地区是中国最干旱的地区之一。艾丁湖夏季最高温度曾达50.6℃，每年40℃以上的高温天气平均在30天以上，8级以上的大风在各风口每年达100天以上。但年降水量却在17毫米以下，蒸发量年平均在3000毫米左右。在这里一般的渠道难以顺利将山上的水引入下游灌溉农田，而坎儿井正适应了这一地区的特点。

坎儿井这种古老的灌溉方式，与其他灌溉形式相比有很多优点：结构简单，无需动力提灌设备，可形成常年不断的自流水；冬暖夏凉，清澈如镜，水质矿化度低；水在地下流动，防止了强烈蒸发，在吐鲁番这个特殊高温地区保持稳定水量，不受气候干旱影响。

坎儿井井口

The mouth of karez

The region of Turpan is one of the hottest and driest regions in China. The temperature of Aiting Lake in summer once reached 50.6°Cand every year the average number of days when the temperature is above 40°C is over 30 and the number of days when the wind is around gale force is over 100. However the yearly rainfall there is below 17 mm and the yearly evaporation amount is about 3,000 mm. In such regions it is very difficult for common canals to draw water from the mountains to irrigate farm land, while a karez is adapted for this purpose.

A Karez is a very ancient irrigation method and has many advantages compared with other irrigation methods. The structure is simple, motor powered irrigation equipment is unnecessary and the water flows automatically and unceasingly year in and year out. It is warm in winter and cool in summer and the water is as clear as a mirror and the degree of mineralization is low. As the water is running underground strong evaporation is prevented and the amount of water is kept stable. This is particularly true in Turpan which is a special high-temperature region and would otherwise not be able to maintain a freshwater supply because of the extreme dryness of the climate.

坎儿井水养育的村庄

A village with karez

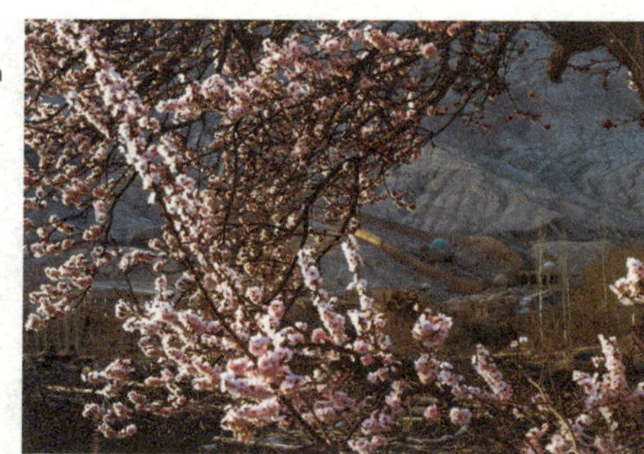

坎儿井浇灌的杏花盛开

Apricot flowers irrigated with karez water are in full bloom

坎儿井灌溉的绿洲

Oasis irrigated with karez water

坎儿井开挖的原始状况示意图
The schematic diagram of how to digging out karez originally

坎儿井博物馆
Karez Museum

参观过坎儿井的人，无不为它构思的巧妙而赞叹。就说它的工程的艰巨性吧，坎儿井甚至能与万里长城、京杭大运河相媲美。那么，坎儿井是怎样造出来的呢?

首先，根据耕地或拟垦荒地位置，向上游寻找水源井估计潜流水水位的埋深，确定坎儿井的布置。根据可能穿过的土层性质，考虑暗渠的适宜纵坡。开挖暗渠，一般从下游开始。先挖明渠的首段和坎儿井的龙口，然后向上游逐段布置竖井。每挖好一个竖井，就从竖井的底部向上游或下游单向或双向逐段挖通暗渠。最后再从头至尾修正暗渠的纵坡。

Everyone who has visited a karez is in admiration for its ingenious design. In the respect of its construction a karez can compare favorably even with the Great Wall and the Great Beijing-Hangzhou Grand Canal. The next question this poses is how do you build one?

First a water source must be found in the upper reaches according to the position of the land that is going to be opened up and the depth of the water table must then be estimated. After that the arrangement of the Karez has to be fixed. The vertical slope of the underground canals must be arranged in accordance with the layers of soil that it might penetrate. The work of digging out the underground canals usually starts from the down reaches. First dig out the head section of the ground canals and the mouth of the karez and then arrange vertical wells to the upper reaches one by one. After digging out a vertical well one-way or two-way underground canals must be dug out at the bottom of the well to the upper or lower reaches, one section after the other. Finally correct the vertical slope of the underground canals from head to end.

坎儿井博物馆的木轮桥

Wooden-wheel bridge at Karez Museum

In the course of digging out the underground canals there is only room for one person at a time and the light is normally provided by oil lamps. Two oil lamps are hung on the vertical well to confirm the direction and the direction and vertical slope of the underground canal was corrected according to the direction and height of the two lamps. Sometimes people used a sunlight reflector to confirm the direction and illuminate their work.

Origin of Karez

There are over 1,000 karezes in the region of Turpan and 436 of them are in Turpan County, almost half of the total number. In Shanshan County there are 396 karezes. The least number of karezes are in Toksun County but that number is still over 160. The total amount of water run out of these karezes reaches more than 500 million cubic meters, exceeding the total volume of the water system in Flaming Mountain.

由于挖暗渠时，一处只能容一人施工，又是在黑暗中摸索，仅靠油灯照明。其定向方法主要是在竖井内垂挂两盏油灯，以这两盏灯的方向和高低，校正暗渠的方向和纵坡。也有用太阳反射镜来定向，并作照明用的。

坎儿井的起源

吐鲁番地区的坎儿井有1000余道，吐鲁番县有436道，差不多占了1／2。鄯善县有396道；托克逊县坎儿井数量最少，但也有160道之多。这些坎儿井的年总出水量达5亿立方米以上，超过了火焰山水系的总流量。

原始的开挖坎儿井的工具模型

Imitation of ancient tools used to build karez

目前关于坎儿井的起源说共有三种意见：

一是来源于汉代（前206–公元220）的井渠。其代表人物是中国近代著名学者王国维，他根据《史记·河渠书》和《大宛列传》中的相关记载，判断坎儿井是秦汉（前221–公元220）时期从中国内地引进的。

二是坎儿井来源于波斯（伊朗）说。根据是：波斯是拥有坎儿井最多的国家。历史已有2000年。坎儿井是随着伊斯兰教的传播而进入新疆的。立此论者说，新疆地名中有个“波斯坎”。但据考察，波斯坎在泽普县，正好在叶尔羌河边，境内不缺水，水位又高，要坎儿井干什么？还有一说，说是巴基斯坦、阿富汗、土耳其和原苏联都把坎儿井叫作“Kariz”，所以坎儿井应是由波斯而来的。但波斯最早的叫法却不是“Kariz”，所以这种说法显然缺乏根据。

坎儿井宾馆　Karez hotel

At present there are three different opinions on the origins of the karezes.

The first is that they originated from the well canal in the Han Dynasty (206 B.C.—220 AD). A famous latter-day scholar in China Wang Guowei holds this opinion. According to the relevant records in *The Book of Rivers and Canals of the Historical Records* and in the *Biographies of Dayuan*, he estimated that the karez was introduced from the hinterland of China during the Qin and Han dynasties (221 B.C. -A.D. 220).

The second is that the karez originated in Persia (Iran). The grounds for this opinion are that Persia is the country with the most karezes and has a history of over 2,000 years. The Karez was introduced to Xinjiang with the spread of Islamic. People holding this opinion say that among the place names in Xinjiang there is one named “Bosika”. But according to investigation, Bosika is within the territory of Zepu County, just along the Yerqiang River. This place does not lack water and the water level there is high, so what is the necessity of having a karez? There is another story: A Karez is called a “Kariz” in Pakistan, Afghan, Turkey and Former Soviet Union, so the karez might have been introduced from Persia. But in Persia the earliest name for it was not “Kariz”, so the ground is not tenable for this opinion.

游客参观坎儿井　Tourists are visiting karez

坎儿井蓄水池边的节日　Celebrations by the reservoir of karez

涝坝水

The reservoir

用坎儿井水制做土陶
Making clay pottery with water from karez

沙漠中靠地下坎儿井水份生长的植物
Desert plants absorb water from karez

三是坎儿井为新疆当地人民所创造。根据是：吐鲁番夏季炎热，年平均降水量仅约20毫米，如果没有人工灌溉，完全不能耕种。怎么办？修明渠，没那个能力，只有修暗渠才可引来地下潜流。再者，新疆人早已有掏泉引水经验。所以，坎儿井其实是掏泉演变而来的。

吐鲁番的坎儿井在历史上有两次大规模的发展，其代表人物一是林则徐；二是左宗棠。

林则徐开拓坎儿井，重点在托克逊县西40里的伊拉里克，其政绩是垦地0.73万公顷。

左宗棠开拓坎儿井，当在清光绪六年（1880年）平定阿古柏叛乱之后，共开凿坎儿井185道。清末民国初，吐鲁番坎儿井多淤塞，农业很少有进展。吐鲁番水贵如油，种麦17日浇一次水，种棉26日浇一次水。有坎儿井一道，每日售水得价银50两之多。为摆脱这种局面，这期间修理雅尔湖原有官坎5道，兴建了干沟坎儿井，修复义学官废坎儿井一道，兴建东坎尔坎儿井，整修了雅尔崖子三道沟、四道沟坎儿井。

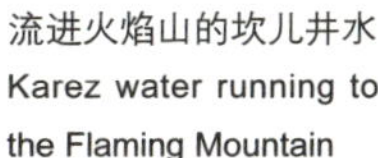

流进火焰山的坎儿井水
Karez water running to the Flaming Mountain

The third is that the karez was created by the local people in Xinjiang. The basis for this is: in the summer it is torrid in Turpan where the annual average rainfall is only about 20 mm. Farming is completely impossible without artificial irrigation. What shall they do? It was impossible to build ground canals and only underground canals can draw underground water. Moreover, Xinjiang people have had the experience of drawing out springs to channel water. So the karez evolved from drawing out springs.

The karez in Turpan experienced large-scale development on two different occasions. The two people responsible for these occasions are Lin Zexu and Zuo Zongtang.

Lin Zexu carved out karezes and attached importance to Yilalik, 40 miles away from Toksun County in the west. His achievement was the reclamation of 7,300 hectares of land.

After putting down the Agobo Rebellion, in the sixth year (1880) of the reign of Emperor Guangxu of the Qing Dynasty, Zuo Zongtang exploited karezes. He carved out 185 karezes altogether. At the end of the Qing Dynasty and during the early years of the Republic of China, most of the karezes in Turpan were silted up and agriculture made little progress. In Turpan water became as precious as oil. As for wheat, people would water it once every 17 days and as for cotton people would water it once every 26 days. A karez could gain more than 50 taels for selling water every day. In order to redeem the situation during that period 5 former official karezes in Yar Lake were repaired, Gangou karez was built, a wasted official karez was renovated in Yixue, Tungkar karez was built and the Santaogou and Sitaogou karezes in Yaryazi were rebuilt.

冬日的坎儿井水是温水　The water in karez is warm during the winter time

坎儿井边上的麦西莱甫　Mexrep by the karez

1949年中华人民共和国成立后，坎儿井的开发和利用进入一个新的阶段。1957年以前，坎儿井的总引水量达到3.67亿立方米，占总引水量的66.7%。1978年中国实行改革开放政策以后，经济发展迅速，科学技术进步明显，人们开始用兴建水库、修明渠（防渗渠）、打机井等现代引水方式灌溉农田，坎儿井的作用逐步减小。坎儿井的引水方法过于原始且成本过高、速度较慢逐渐处于次要地位。目前，吐鲁番有许多坎儿井已经干涸，仅占实际利用水量的24%　。

也许有一天坎儿井会彻底失去它的效能，但作为一种文化遗产，它必将永远矗立在大地，见证着人类文明的发展。

After the founding of the People's Republic of China in 1949, the development and exploitation of the karezes entered a new stage. Before 1957 the total water volume drawn by karezes reached 367 million cubic meters, occupying 66.7 percent of the total volume of drawn water. After the adoption of reforms and the opening up policy in 1978 the economy developed fast. Science and technology made obvious progress, people started to adopt modern ways of drawing water for irrigation such as reservoirs, ground canals (infiltration-prevention canals) and motor-pumped wells and the karez played a less important role. The method of drawing water in a karez is too rude, the cost is too high and the speed is relatively slow, so it gradually became inferior. At present many karezes in Turpan have dried up and the water drawn by them only occupies 24 percent of the actual volume of exploited water.

Maybe one day the karez will lose its efficiency completely, but as a cultural heritage, it will certainly stand up to witness the development of human culture.

巨大的工程——坎儿井

自天山或喀拉乌成山区奔腾而下的湍急水流，出山后不久，就很快消失了。它们大多不能流到适宜人类居住、生活的黄土地带，就已大部分渗漏在戈壁砾石之中，转化为地下的潜流。要取得这些水源，保护这些珍贵的水源不被沙砾吸收，就必须修建防渗、防冲渠道。但这种像凹底锅一样的地形地势，地面坡降很大，水势十分湍急。修建的明渠，防冲、防渗的要求很高。没有十分坚固的，长达数10千米的渠道，就不能将水引到绿洲农耕地带。这在古代，当然不是很容易实现的工程。而如果利用盆地地形及下流的水势，修建暗渠，使地下潜水顺一条人工的、相对比较平缓的渠道下流到盆地深处，就可以很方便的将水引出地面。

挖坎儿井用具
A tool used to build karez

挖坎儿井时，井口的辘轳向上提泥
In building karez, people use a windlass to lift earth

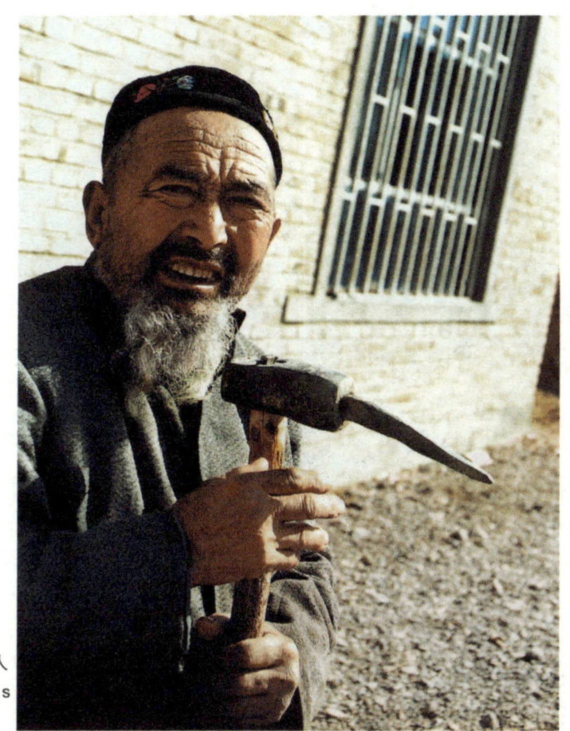

挖坎儿井的老人
An old man is building karez

Grand Project—Karez

The turbulent waters running down from Tianshan Mountain and Kalawucheng Mountain disappear soon after running out of the mountains. Most of the waters infiltrates into the Gobi gravels and transforms to underground streams before running to the loess zones where many people reside and live. Canals had to be built to prevent infiltration and to stop all the precious water from being absorbed by the gravel. But in hilly terrain, the slopes are very severe, and the flows are consequently very turbulent. Such ground canals are not easy to build. Nothing but a very solid canal scores of kilometers long is sufficient to draw water to faraway farmland. In ancient times such construction was of course a very challenging project. However, it was convenient to draw water out of the ground to build underground canals by taking advantages of the terrain of the basin and the downward flow of water, where the underground water could run down to the depth of the basin along an artificial and comparatively gentle canal.

坎儿井是一种地下暗渠，它将水引向盆地深处进行自流灌溉。在这一工程中，主要的设施是一个个竖井及连通竖井之间的地下渠道。有经验的水工选择地下水溢出地带，依次开凿竖井，利用竖井作为出口，掏挖地下暗渠。竖井、暗渠，自然也成了吸引、汇聚戈壁砾石层中点滴渗水的工具。每隔二三十米掏挖竖井一口，彼此之间暗渠相通。这样，坎儿井沿线，四周沙砾中的渗水，都可以不断被吸收进来。地下水愈汇愈多，愈向盆地深处延伸，竖井也愈来愈浅。地势高处最深的竖井，可以深到六七十米，而到出水口的附近，竖井就差不多接近地面了。这一地段的竖井，它的作用和山前地段的竖井也不一样了。因为竖井很浅，达不到地下水的含水层，它自然也就失掉了汇聚地下水的功能，而只剩下了输水的作用。直到盆地深处，地下渠道已到达地面，这时，不用任何提水工具，清澈、洁净的地下水一年到头都可以源源不断缓缓流出地面，汇向一个个储水的涝坝。

下井(吐鲁番挖坎儿井)

Getting down the well to build karez in Turpan

清上来的泥土
Earth is lifted from underground

Karez is an underground canal which can draw water to the depth of the basin for automatic irrigation. In this project the major installations are vertical wells and the underground canals connecting these wells. Experienced water workmen carefully select the places where underground water could spill out to dig a series of vertical wells. They use the vertical wells to dig out underground canals. And the vertical wells and underground canals of course became the perfect tools to draw and gather the drops of infiltrated water in layers of gravel in the Gobi. Every twenty or thirty meters they would dig out a vertical well and underground canals would connect these vertical wells. So along the karez the infiltrated water in the surrounding gravel could be continuously drawn. As the underground water gathers and runs down further and further to the depth of the basin, the vertical wells become shallower and shallower. In places of high terrain the furthest vertical well could be as deep as sixty or seventy meters; while nearby the exit of water, the vertical wells are almost close to ground level. The vertical wells in such areas play a different role from that of the vertical wells in the areas before mountains. As the vertical wells are very shallow, they can not access the water table underground and thus naturally lose the function of gathering underground water. They can only transport the water until the depth of the basin allows the underground canal to reach the ground. Then there is no need to fetch the water and the clear and clean underground water can run out of the ground in great volume and can fill many dams in order to store water.

吐鲁番盆地的地下水资源的源头天山冰川融化水
Glacier meltwater, the source of the largest underground water in Turpan Basin

这样的坎儿井，一般长度有三四千米，也有长达10千米以上的。水通过坎儿井天然的过滤，水质良好，而且冬暖夏凉，不论人畜饮用还是农田灌溉都十分理想。在吐鲁番盆地这样一处十分干燥的高温地带，水源是极其珍贵的，坎儿井工程使水源得到了最大程度地利用，而且防止了水量的强烈蒸发。

坎儿井工程是十分艰巨的。掏挖一口深数10米的竖井，出土量就有上百甚至数百立方米。一条坎儿井，有数十、上百座竖井。加上绵延数千米的地下渠道，该是多大的土方工程。而在遥远的古代，这些土石都得靠人的两手，一锹一镐挖出，一筐一筐提起。惟一的机械，就是一具辘轳。只从吐鲁番盆地说，这1000条左右的坎儿井，仅地下渠道的长度最少也要在3000千米以上，加上竖井，这是怎样浩大的工程！

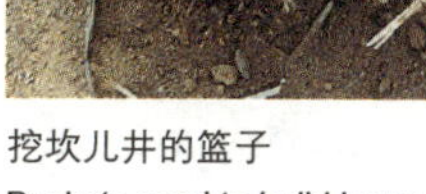

挖坎儿井的篮子
Baskets used to build karez

井下挖泥
Digging in the underground of karez

This kind of karez is usually as long as three or four km, sometimes even extending to over 10 km. After the natural filtration effected by karezes, the water has a very good quality. Furthermore, it is warm in winter and cool in summer, so it is ideal both for human and animal drinking and for irrigation for farm land. In the Turpan Basin where it is very dry and the temperature is very high, water is extremely precious and karez engineering makes full use of the largest water sources prevents loss of water through evaporation.

Karez engineering is quite complex. The volume of dug-out soil for a vertical well with a depth of scores of meters is more than a hundred or even hundreds of cubic meters. One karez has scores of or hundreds of vertical wells in addition to the underground canals extending for many kilometers. It is quite an amazing piece of work. In ancient times the earth and stones had to be dug out by hand by workers with shovel and pick and carried with baskets. The unique machine was a windlass. In respect of Turpan Basin, these 1,000 odd karezes had underground canals with a total length of at least 3,000 km in addition to many vertical wells. What an absolutely stunning piece of engineering!

从帕孜克里克千佛洞流过的坎儿井明渠

Water running through the ground canals by the Bezklik Thousand Buddha Cave

Evolution of the Name of Karez

Karez is called Qanat in Iran, Madazcha in Iraq and Kariz in Turpan, and their pronunciations are distinctively different. In China the word karez first appeared in the time of the Spring and Autumn Period and the Warring States Period. In the Xizhou document from the Tang Dynasty there were records of "Huma well canals". In the third year (1575) of the Wanli Period of the Ming Dynasty, in *Distant Foreigners Thank the Emperor for His Favor and Ask for Tribute* by Shi Maohua, there were records of "Yakan'er". Until the time of the Qing Emperor Qianlong (1736-1795) it was known as "Kajin".

It can be concluded with great certainty that the name karez originated in China. The way it evolved is as follows: well (in Chinese: Jing) (Zhou Dynasty) → Kan well (kanjing) (from the Warring States Period to Han Dynasty) → well canal (jing qu) (the Tang and Yuan dynasties) → ka well (kajing) (the Qing Dynasty) → karez (in Chinese: kan'erjing) (contemporary times)

坎儿井名称的演变

坎儿井，伊朗称之为Qanat，伊拉克称作Madazcha，而吐鲁番则称作kariz，三者读音显然不一样。在中国，坎儿井一词最早出现于春秋战国时期。《庄子·秋水篇》中曾有"子独不闻夫坎井之蛙乎"之句。唐代西州文书中有"胡麻井渠"的记载。明代万历三年（公元1575年），石茂华《远夷谢恩求贡事》一文中有关于"牙坎儿"的记载。到了清朝乾隆年间（1736—1795）则称之为"卡井"。

由此可知，坎儿井名称源自中国。它演变的过程可归纳为井（周）→坎井（战国至汉）→井渠（唐、元）→卡井（清）→坎儿井（现代）。

天山冰川　Glacier in the Tianshan Mountain

坎儿井明渠　Ground canal of karez

坎儿井暗渠　Underground canal of karez

室内的竖井　An indoor vertical well

坎儿井暗渠　Underground canals of karez

坎儿井的命名方式

吐鲁番地区的坎儿井都有自己的名字。其命名方式多种多样，不拘一格。

1、以掘井人姓名命名。如“杨西成坎儿孜”、“何元坎儿孜”、“艾提巴克坎儿孜”。

2、以动植物名称命名。如“尤勒滚坎儿孜”（尤勒滚，维吾尔语，红柳之意）、“提开坎儿孜”（提开，维吾尔语，公山羊之意）。

3、以地名、地理方位命名。如“吐尔坎儿孜”（吐尔，维吾尔语，烽火台，因井旁有烽火台，故名）、“边西坎儿孜”（边西，维吾尔语，地名）。

4、以水的味道命名。如“西喀力克坎儿孜”（西喀力克，维吾尔语，甘甜）、“阿其克坎儿孜”（阿其克，维吾尔语，苦味）。

5、以职务、职业命名。如“吉力力团长坎儿孜”、“木匠坎儿孜”、“醋房坎儿孜”等。

遗弃的坎儿井井口
A deserted karez mouth

The Way in which Karez's are named

The karezes in the Turpan Region all have their own names. The ways in which they are named are various and don't stick to one particular pattern.

1. Named after the persons digging out the wells, such as “Yang Xicheng Karez”, “He Yuan Karez” and “Atibake Karez”.

2. Named after animals or plants, such as “Yolergun Karez” (Yolergunis a Uygur word meaning ‘red willow’) and “Tiki Karez” (Tikiis a Uygur word meaning ‘male goat’).

3. Named after places or geographic direction and positions, such as “Tur Karez” (Turis a Uygur word meaning ‘beacon tower’, as there is a beacon tower beside it from which it took its name) and “Bensi Karez” (Bensi is a Uygur word meaning the name of a place.)

4. Named after the taste of water, such as “Xikalik Karez” (Xikalik is a Uygur word meaning sweet) and “Achik Karez” (Achik is a Uygur word meaning bitter).

5. Named after jobs and occupations, such as “Chilili – “Regimental Commander Karez”, “Carpenter Karez” and even “Vinegar House Karez”, etc.

坎儿井之最

最长的坎儿井是鄯善县红土坎儿孜。该坎儿井在鄯善葡萄开发公司东1．5千米处，全长25千米，日浇地4公顷左右。

最短的坎儿井是吐鲁番市艾丁湖乡阿其克村的阿山尼牙孜坎儿孜，全长仅150米，日水量浇地667平方米。

竖井最深的坎儿井是鄯善吐峪沟乡苏贝希坎村东部的努尔买提主任坎儿孜，全长20.7千米、井深98米，日浇地1.67公顷，开凿于1900年。

水量最大的坎儿井是吐鲁番市艾丁湖乡吾力托尔坎村欧吐拉坎儿孜，日水量浇地4.7公顷。

Tops of Karez

The longest karez is the Laterite Karez in Shanshan County. It is 1.5 km away from Shanshan Grapes Development Company in the east, it is 25 km long and provides irrigation for 4-hectares of farmland per day.

The shortest karez is the Ashanniyazi Karez in Achik Village, Aiting Lake Township in Turpan City. It is only 150 meters long and irrigates a 667-square-meter area of farmland per day.

The karez with the deepest vertical well is the Director Normati Karez in the east of Subisika Village, Tuyugou Township in Shangshang. It is 20.7 km long and the depth of the well is 98 meters. Dug out in 1900, it irrigates a 1.67-hectare area of farmland per day.

The karez with the highest water volume is the Otola Karez in Olitorka Village, Aiting Lake Township in Turpan City. It irrigates a 4.7-hectare area of farmland per day.

戈壁上的坎儿井涝坝（晾水池）。坎儿井水流出后经太阳晒再浇田才好（左）
The reservoir (sunning water pool) of karez in gobi. It is good for farming that water is running through karez and sunning before irrigation (left)

原始的挖井辘轳（右）
An ancient windlass to build karez (right)

水量最小的坎儿井是吐鲁番市牙儿乡伊里木村西面的克其尔坎儿孜，全长300米，日水量浇地0.04公顷。

最古老的坎儿井是在火焰山的胜金口水库西坝端一古城遗址附近发现的。遗址东有一古墓群，在水库附近曾挖出两个陶坛和一陶碗，据鉴定，是魏晋（220–420）时期的文物。这条坎儿井长约100米，出口处距古墓处仅有30米，古井有7个竖井，每个竖井相隔约10米，现已干涸，出口处有一段已坍塌成明渠。古井周围并无任何耕地，仅有这一处古城。据分析，这是一处由掏泉形成的坎儿井，它的用途是给古城供应生活用水。这是吐鲁番至今已发现的年代最远的坎儿井遗址，距今约1500年。

The karez with the lowest water volume is the Kerqir Karez in the west of Yilimo Village, Ya'er Township in Turpan City. It is 300 meters long and irrigates a 0.04-hectare area of farmland per day.

The oldest karez is found near the historical site of an ancient town at the west end of the Shinchinko Reservoir Dam in Flaming Mountain. There is an ancient group of graves on the east of the site and two ceramic jugs and one ceramic bowl were excavated near the reservoir. According to archaeologists, they are cultural relics of the Wei and Jin periods (220-420). This karez is about 100 meters long. The exit is only 30 meters away from the ancient graves. The ancient karez has 7 vertical wells and the distance between every two vertical wells is about 10 meters. They had dried up and a section near the exit had collapsed into a ground canal. Around the ancient karez there is no farmland but only the ancient town. According to analysis it is a karez formed from drawing out springs. It was used to provide the ancient town with drinking water. It is the site of the karez with the longest history of about 1,500 years among the excavated karezes in Turpan.

储水池，井口的必备

Reservoir, a necessary part of karez mouth

坎儿井“龙口”
The Dragon Mouth of karez

清理明渠
Cleaning up the ground canals

井水浇出又一春
A new spring has come

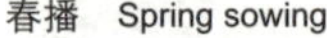
春播　Spring sowing

老坎儿井　Ancient karez

历史上哈密回王的“鸽子坎儿井”遗迹

The historical relic of the Pigeon Karez built by Uygur Kings

从火焰山底部流出的坎儿井明渠

Ground canals passing through the foot of the Flaming Mountain

特克斯八卦城

BAGUA (EIGHT DIAGRAMS) TOWN

八卦城全景
The panorama of Bagua Town

八卦城石刻
Stone inscription in Bagua Town

八卦城牌坊
Memorial archway in Bagua Town

八卦城

在美丽的天山北麓，存在着一个世界上最大、最完整的八卦城，它就是特克斯县城。特克斯县城以其街道形式独特、城区规划奇异而闻名遐迩，被誉为“八卦城”，其独特的八卦建筑布局已载入上海大世界吉尼斯之最，2004年又被新疆维吾尔自治区人民政府命名为“历史文化名城”。

On the northern side of the Tianshan Mountains sits the county seat of Tek. It is the world's largest and most complete Bagua Town. Its unique octagonal layout, which was modeled on the eight-diagram pattern, gained it a place in the Shanghai World Guinness Record. In 2004, it was listed as a historic and cultural city by the provincial government of the Xinjiang Uygur Autonomous Region.

八卦城——环内的广场
The plaza in the 1st ring road of Bagua Town

阴阳柱
Yin Yang Column

特克斯县石人　Stone Statues in Tekes County

街心广场　Plaza

神秘的西部小城

这里是一个"天地交而万物通，上下交而万物同"的地方。

这里是历史上塞种、月氏、乌孙、回纥、突厥、蒙古、柯尔克孜、哈萨克、维吾尔、汉等22个民族的人民都曾繁衍生息的地方。

这里是中国道家文化传播最西端的地方，也是世界上惟一的乌孙文化与易经文化交织的地方。

这里是中国历史上第一位和亲公主——汉代的细君公主生活的地方，也是中国古代汉王朝与西域游牧古国和亲时间最长、来往最密切的地方。

……

A Mysterious City in West China

Tek is an ideal place in terms of fengshui according to Book of Changes (or I Ching). A total of 22 ethnic groups, including the Saka, Indoscythae, Usun, Uigur, Turk, Mongolian, Kirghiz, Kazak, Uygur and Han have lived in this area during the passage of history.

As the place farthest west in China that China's Taoism culture has reached, it is the only place in the world, which witnesses an integration of the Usun culture and the I-ching culture. As the first princess in Chinese history who was married to a foreign leader on the basis of political objectives, Princess Xijun of the Han Dynasty (205 BC - 220 AD) lived here for many years. Compared with other nomadic tribes in the Western Regions, the Wusun kept a longer and closer relationship with the Han court.

八卦城中心塔　The Central Tower of Bagua Town

The State of Usun in the History

Tek was home to the state of Usun which was the most powerful in the Western Regions of China in ancient times. The earliest historical records related to the nomadic tribe can be found in *Historical Records: Dayuan*, a great work of history written by Sima Qian of the Western Han Dynasty (206BC-25AD).

At that time, the Han Dynasty was threatened by the Huns (or the Huns). Emperor Wudi (157 BC - 87 BC)of the Han Dynasty decided to send Zhang Qian as an envoy to the Western Regions, seeking an alliance with the Usun to in order to counter the Xiongnu threat. After meeting with Zhang Qian, Mokun, king of the state of Usun, believed that it was good for his country to establish a marriage relationship with the rich and powerful Han Dynasty. Therefore, he chose over 1,000 fine horses as a gift for Emperor Wudi.

历史上的乌孙

特克斯是历史上中国西域最大游牧古国——乌孙国的所在地。西汉（前206—公元25）的司马迁在《史记·大宛列传》中最早记载了乌孙国的情况。

当时，为了减轻匈奴对汉朝的威胁，汉武帝（前157—前87）派张骞出使西域，希望联盟乌孙牵制匈奴。乌孙王莫昆接见张骞后，认为同国力强盛而富有的汉朝联姻，也会使乌孙的繁荣得到保障，于是便向汉武帝献了1000多匹乌孙骏马。

八卦城中心塔石刻
Stone inscriptions at the Central Tower of Bagua Town

此前，汉武帝翻开《易经》占卜得到的卦上说：“神马当从西北来。”得到乌孙骏马后，汉武帝十分高兴，将乌孙马命名为“天马”，（后来武帝见大宛国进献的汗血马更为雄健，遂将乌孙马更名为“西极”，把“天马”改赐给了大宛马。）并把江都王刘建之女刘细君作为公主嫁给了乌孙王。乌孙王也在特克斯专门修建“夏都”宫殿，按乌孙和汉朝习俗隆重迎娶了细君公主。

特克斯县八卦公园　Bagua Park, Tekes County

特克斯县八卦公园内周文王像
The statue of King Wen of Zhou at Bagua Park, Tekes County

Before this, Emperor Wudi had gained an insight from Book of Changes that “Divine Horse shall come from the northwest.” When obtaining the fine horses from the Usun, the delighted emperor styled them “Heavenly Horses”. (Later when even stronger Blood-Sweater horses were obtained from the state of Dayuan he renamed horses from Usun “Horses of the Far West”, and reserved the name “Heavenly Horses” for those from the Dayuan.) Meanwhile, he ordered Liu Xijun, the daughter of the king of Jiandu, Liu Jian, as a princess to marry the king of the state of Usun. The Usun king had a palace built for Princess Xijun in Tek and a grand wedding ceremony was held according to the local customs and the customs of the Han Dynasty.

细君公主是中国历史上第一位和亲的公主，她还被称作过“江都公主”、“乌孙公主”。由于出生在江南水乡江苏扬州，长在长安皇宫，肤色白净，花容月貌，因此她又被乌孙人称作过“柯木孜公主”，意为“肤色白净美丽得像马奶酒”。作为一个柔弱女子，她化干戈为玉帛，心系国之安危，为多民族国家的团结和融合，为西域安定以及人民免遭涂炭做出了巨大贡献，被称为西汉与乌孙友好的和亲大使。

在细君公主去世后继续承担和亲重任的是楚王刘戊的孙女解忧公主。解忧公主嫁到乌孙后，深得乌孙人民爱戴，被尊称为“乌孙国母”。

Princess Xijun, also known as Princess Jiangdu or Princess Wusun, is the first princess to be married to a foreign leader for political motives in Chinese history. She was born in Yangzhou of Jiangsu Province, a water-rich area in south China and grew up in the royal palace in Chang'an, the capital of the Han Dynasty. After she got to the Wusun, the people there gave the beautiful princess the name of Princess Koumiss for her fair complexion. As a delicate lady, she managed to maintain a friendly relationship between the Usun and the Han court, thus famed as a peaceful emissary between the two states. What she did brought stability and peace for the peoples in the Western Regions and the Central Plain during that period. This helped promote unity and integrity among the different ethnic groups in the country.

After Princess Xijun died, Princess Jieyou, the granddaughter of the king of Chu, Liu Wu, became another princess to be married into the Usun. She also won the respect of the Usun people and was called “the mother of the Usun”.

八卦城介绍碑
Stone tablet introducing Bagua Town

兑街——乾街二环民族食品馕
Dui Street to Qian Street, 2nd ring road: local food Kao Nang (roasted Nang)

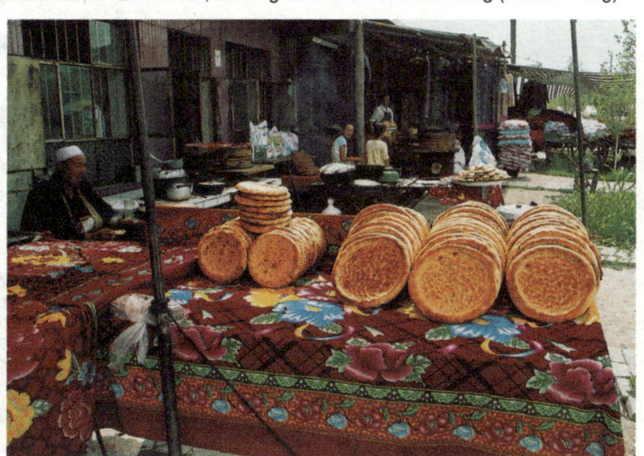

兑街——乾街二环民族手工艺品
Dui Street to Qian Street, 2nd ring road: local handcrafts

兑街（阿克奇街）是八卦城的商业街
Dui Street (Akeqi Street) is the commercial street in Bagua Town

艮街（即阔克阿尕什街）位于县城东北方
Gen Street (Kuokeagashi Street) is in the north of the Town

冯嫽是西汉与乌孙友好关系中不得不提的一个重要人物。她是解忧公主的侍者，嫁给了乌孙右大将。她“尝持汉节为公主使”，亲自走访附近一些国家，当地人民尊敬地称她为“冯夫人”。为巩固乌孙王权，她还先后两次往返长安与乌孙国之间。冯嫽堪称中国历史上第一位杰出的女外交家，也是当时的女政治家。

汉宣帝（前91—前49）时，乌孙国已归汉朝的西域都护府管辖。

Feng Liao was a lady-in-waiting of Princess Jieyou and later became the wife of a Usun general. She played an important role in the Usun-Han relationship. On behalf of Princess Jieyou, Feng once visited a number of countries in Western Regions and enjoyed high prestige among these states, and was thus addressed as “Madame Feng”. Working as an emissary of the Han Dynasty, she successfully defused an internal crisis in Usun. Feng, a woman politician at that time, is really worthy of the title of the first outstanding woman diplomat in Chinese history.

During the period of Emperor Xuandi (91 BC - 49 BC) of the Han Dynasty, Usun was under the administration of the Western Regions Protectorate of the Han Dynasty.

八卦城之由来

特克斯八卦城建立于民国时期（1912—1949），但其最原始的雏形据说形成于南宋时期（1127—1279）。

据传，当时道教全真七子之一、龙门派教主“长春真人”丘处机应成吉思汗的邀请，前往西域指教治国扶民方略和长生不老之道。他用了三年时间西游天山，被途中特克斯河谷的集山之刚气、川之柔顺、水之盛脉为一体的景象打动，于是就以这里作为“八卦城”的风水核心，确定了坎北、离南、震东、兑西四个方位。从此，这里就成特克斯八卦城最原始的雏形。特克斯也由此成为中国道家文化传播最西端的地方。

巽街（阿热勒街）位于县城东南

Xun Street (Arele Street) is in the southeast of the Town

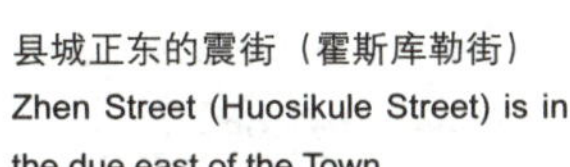

县城正东的震街（霍斯库勒街）

Zhen Street (Huosikule Street) is in the due east of the Town

Origins of the Bagua (Eight Diagrams) Town

The Bagua Town of Tek was built during the period of the Republic of China (1912-1949). However, it is said that the formation of its original design should be dated from the Southern Song Dynasty (1127-1276).

Legend has it that at that time Qiu Chuji accepted Genghis Khan's invitation to go to the Western Regions. Qiu Chuji was one of the seven master disciples of the Ch'uan-chen Taoism and abbot of the Dragon Gate Sect. The purpose of his journey to the west was to teach the first emperor of the Yuan Dynasty (1271-1368) how to run the country well and provide peace and security and how to nurture the people. During his long expedition, Qiu spent three years visiting the Tianshan Mountains. When he reached the Tek River valley, he was deeply impressed by the lofty mountains and the turbulent river. As a master of Zhouyi,he then decided on four directions, namely, Kan in the north, Li in the south, Zhen in the east and Tui in the west on the basis of Eight Trigrams. The Tek River valley was chosen as the core of the Bagua Town in terms of fengshui. It thus should be the place where the earliest design of the Bagua Town of Tek stood and Tek became the western end of the influence of Taoism culture.

位于震街——巽街之间的康之源大药房
Kang Zhi Yuan drug store located between the Zhen Street and the Xun Street

坎街——艮街之间的新奇大楼
New building between the Kan Street and the Gen Street

1936年冬天，当时新疆的国民党军阀盛世才的岳父邱宗浚调任伊犁屯垦使兼警备司令后，亲临特克斯查勘时发现了这一雏形。邱宗浚素来喜欢《老子》、《庄子》和《周易》，并精通“易”理。他认为八卦城城址集中了“易”理的优越条件，算得上是一块风水宝地。于是，取《周易》中“天地交而万物通，上下交而其志同”的意境，设计了八卦格局城区建设图。1939年，第二任特克斯县长班吉春依据邱宗浚的规划蓝图择地兴建新城。当时，班吉春还请来俄罗斯专家帮助测量，打桩放线。

In the winter of 1936, Qiu Zongjun discovered the octagonal layout left through the ages when he did surveys in Tek. Qiu was the commander of the troops stationed to open up the wasteland and guard the security of Yili area. He was also the father-in-law of Sheng Shicai, a warlord occupying the vast Xinjiang region. Qiu Zongjun always liked reading the ancient Chinese classics, such as *Lao Tzu*, *Zhuangzi* and *Zhouyi* and had a good command of the “yi” theory. He thought that the site of the Bagua Town was really a place with all the favorable geographical conditions in the light of “yi” theory. In line with the theory on heaven and earth in Zhouyi, Qiu designed the city construction map in an eight-diagram pattern. In 1939, the second head of Tek County, Ban Jichun, made Qiu’s design become reality and some Russian experts were asked for help when the construction began.

这座城据《周易》八卦“后天图”设计建造，以方圆28亩的八卦街心公园为中心，以相等间距、用八头牛向八个方向犁了八条线，就是现在八卦城的乾、兑、离、震、巽、坎、艮、坤八条主干道，每隔350米便有一条宽30米的环形大道，每增加一条环形街道，即增加八条射线道，如迷宫一般，64卦街道布局，使整个县城形成路路相通，让神奇的《周易》方位学说以有形的方式展现在世人面前。当年10月新城大样初具，政府便入城办公了。现在共有4道环形大道，32条街道，正向第5环发展。

This town was designed and built on the basis of the Later Heaven System of *Zhouyi*. Centered on the street garden with a diameter of 1.87 hectares, eight straight thoroughfares came from eight equiangular furrows ploughed by eight oxen when the city was built. The eight thoroughfares serve as the eight directions of Eight Diagrams, respectively being the Qian, Tui, Li, Zhen, Xun, Kan, Gen and Kun. They are intersected by a number of 30-meter-wide ring roads at intervals of 350 meters. In this way, when a new ring road is built, eight ray-like streets will be created as a result. The labyrinth of streets actually forms a 64-hexagram pattern. It is all the well-connected streets that make the profound philosophy concept in Zhouyi a true existing entity. The county government moved in the newly-built city when the construction was basically completed in October 1939. At present, there are four ring roads and 32 ray-like streets in the city. The fifth ring road is planned.

县城正南的离街（博斯提街）
Li Street (Bositi Street) is in the due south of the Town

离街——坤街之间的新华书店、邮政局
The Xin Hua bookstore and the post office between the Li Street and the Kun Street

霍斯库勒街（震街）
Huosikule Street (Zhen Street)

Tek Town is a true town of eight-diagram style. What makes it wonderful lies in the perfect practice of Eight Diagrams of *Zhouyi* theory being realized. You have a good understanding of this when you stand on the top of the over-50-meter-high sightseeing tower in the center of the city. Having a bird's-eye view of the surrounding area from this tower, you can see a pattern resembling Eight Diagrams, which is formed by the streets and grasslands. If you have a chance to fly over the city, you will also have a bird's-eye view of the Bagua Town.

特克斯城是一座内含六十四卦"满卦"，386爻"满爻"布局的城市，囊括了《周易》的全部卦爻，是一座真正意义上的八卦城。它的奇妙之处在于把《周易》中64卦、386爻数理完整设计成一个城市，堪称凝固的《周易》。只要一登上城中心50多米高的八卦观光塔，立刻就可以领略其神秘。鸟瞰观光塔下方，青灰色的街道、绿色的草地纵横交错，形如一个八卦勘盆。如果你有机会乘飞机在城市上空经过，那么八卦城的全貌就会尽展在你的眼前。

阿扎提街（坎街） Azati Street (Kan Street)

县城西南的坤街——兑街之间的人民广场
The People´s Square is located between the Kun Street and the Dui Street in the southwest of the Town

特克斯县城背靠连绵起伏、巍峨峻拔的乌孙山，前濒波涛奔涌、带水环回的特克斯河，水草丰茂、地势开阔，环境宜人，再加上神秘的八卦城区和悠久的历史文化，魅力非凡。

The county seat of Tek, situated back against the lofty Wusunshan Mountains, is skirted by the turbulent Tek River. It is blessed with beautiful natural scenery. Due to the mysterious Bagua city and its long history, it becomes even more charming.

县城西南的坤街（阔克街）
Kun Street (Kuoke Street) is in the southwest of the Town

县城正北的坎街（阿扎提街）
Kan Street (Azhati Street) is in the due north of the Town

八卦城之奇

现在，整座体现易经文化内涵和八卦奇特奥秘思想的城镇已初具规模。整个县城呈放射状圆形，街道布局如神奇迷宫般，路路相通、街街相连。

特克斯八卦县城有两奇。

一奇就是这座城市的马路上没有一盏红绿灯。1996年，有关部门、专家和学者都认为，按照县城现有的建设，各道路是环环相连、条条相通的，这对一个县城来说，绝不会产生塞车和堵路的情况，车辆和行人无论从哪个方向都能够通达目的地。于是，道路上的红绿灯都被取消，特克斯也由此成为一座没有红绿灯的城市。

Unique Features of the Bagua Town

Now, the eight-diagram town, emanating a mysterious sense of I-ching culture, has begun to take shape. Its layout is in round with radial patterns. All the streets and roads are well connected.

Tek Town has two unique features.

Firstly, there are no traffic lights in the streets. In 1996, according to the departments, experts and scholars concerned, its well-connected streets would make traffic jams impossible in such a small city. People and vehicles can reach their destinations no matter which way they choose. All the traffic lights were dismantled and Tek became a city with no traffic lights.

县城西北的乾街（古勒巴格街）又名八卦食街
Qian Street (Gulebage Street), in the northwest of the Town, is also known as the food Street

除没有红绿灯外，八卦城还有一奇，就是容易使外地人“转向”。在这方面曾经有过一个笑谈。据说一位外地司机严重超载，车到八卦城后，意识到可能会在街道上碰到交警。于是，他趁夜间选择一条自认为偏僻的道路，绕行到中心八卦文化广场附近。他借助灯光远远看到前方有一位交警在执勤，吓得紧急调头，准备绕过。当他抱着侥幸心理从其他道路绕到前方时，一看前面还是有交警。他又“偷偷摸摸”地从另外的道路绕行，就是躲不开“烦人”的交警。他不信“邪”地继续绕，就这样一次比一次绕得多，一次比一次绕得远，最后究竟绕了多少遍，连他自己都记不清了，这位“糊涂”司机整整绕了一夜。第二天，筋疲力尽的他把自己的“遭遇”讲给同行，结果成了笑谈，并迅速在整个县城传开。其实，这位“晕头转向”的司机，一个夜晚碰到的都是中心八卦文化场路口的那一个交警。

其实，外地人来此看到每条一样的街，难免迷路，只要通过街心路口的各式雕塑就可认清你要去的街道。

In addition to this, the other unique feature is: it is easy for new comers to lose their way in the city. There is an interesting story regarding this. An overloaded truck came here. As a new comer, the driver was afraid of being seized by the traffic police. So he chose a road he thought safe enough and entered the city at night. When traveling to the Bagua Culture Square in the center of the city, he found that there was a traffic policeman on duty ahead. Changing direction immediately, he decided to try another road to avoid the policeman. He tried again and again during the whole night. However, no matter which way he chose, he would always find a traffic policeman standing ahead. In the end, even he himself didn't remember how many ways he had tried. On the second day, the exhausted driver told his experience to other drivers. As a result, the story rapidly spread through the city as a joke. In fact, the confused driver saw only one traffic policeman that night. It is the one who was on duty near the square.

Actually, for any new comer, it is quite possible to be confused and disoriented in the labyrinth of streets. However, by the different statues at the street junctions, you can easily reach your destination.

艮街——震街之间的街景
Street view between Gen Street and Zhen Street

图书在版编目（CIP）数据

中国新疆名胜古迹：汉英对照/余言，向京著；王国振，许华锋译.
——北京：五洲传播出版社，2011.8
ISBN 978-7-5085-2165-7

Ⅰ.①中… Ⅱ.①余… ②向… ③王… ④许…
Ⅲ.①名胜古迹－介绍－新疆－汉、英 Ⅳ.①K928.704.5

中国版本图书馆CIP数据核字(2011)第158908号

总 顾 问：王国庆 胡 伟
总 策 划：郭卫民 李向平
总 监 制：陈文俊 侯汉敏
编　　委：艾力提·沙力也夫 李 洁 刘 江
主　　编：徐醒生

中国新疆名胜古迹（中英对照）

撰　　稿：余 言 向 京
英文翻译：王国振 许华锋
摄　　影：吴凤翔 宋士敬 宋 君 程 春 张永禄 晏 先 韩连赟
张国军 黄永中 康 剑 向 京 新疆龟兹石窟研究所
王 钰 朱明俊 富家力强 刘湘泰 刘灵波
责任编辑：许冬梅
装帧设计：北京嘉悦美印包装有限公司
出版发行：五洲传播出版社
社　　址：北京市北三环中路31号凯奇大厦7层B座
邮政编码：100088
电　　话：0086-10-82000308 82002803
传　　真：0086-10-82005975
印　　刷：北京嘉彩印刷有限公司
开　　本：889×1194 1/24
印　　张：9.5
版　　次：2011年8月第1版 2011年8月第1次印刷
定　　价：160.00元